Praise for *Passing the Test of Faith*

In this good and easy-to-read book, Eddie Johnson shares one of the most difficult challenges that a parent can face. Eddie is very transparent about the difficulties he faced and his faith that helped him overcome what could have taken him out.

Passing the Test of Faith is a thought-provoking book filled with personal stories, which might have you reading your own story. I highly recommend this book to anyone who may be questioning their faith and frankly questioning God.

– Deborah King Halstead

Passing the Test of Faith, grabbed my attention right from the very start. I was intrigued to hear about Eddie's "Faith Walk" and how he was able to develop and maintain his strong relationship with God while managing life's uncertain journey. Eddie is transparent about his life as a man, husband, and father, and even takes us on a journey through his childhood.

In this book, you will receive practical tips on how to grow your faith, methods of effective relationship building, leadership skills, and parenting techniques. It will touch your heart and tickle your funny bone, but most importantly, it will help you grow closer to God while developing your "faith" muscle.

Eddie provides a clear roadmap for navigating "headwinds" that can sabotage our faith and prevent us from walking in our purpose as Christians. This book surely gives us all we need to walk in victory!

nes,
tive

In this book, Eddie shares how he emerged victorious from two tremendous tests by holding fast to his faith... and you can too. As a witness to the biggest faith test Eddie faced in 2003, his faith in God has remained steadfast and amazing. Everyone who reads this book will be blessed, as Eddie shares the important truths he learned through his journey!

– Rev. Ernest Glenn,
West Hunter Street Baptist Church

What do you do when your Lazarus is sick and God shows up at a time that seems to be too late? Even worse, what if he doesn't answer your request for healing, and your Lazarus dies. This is the foundation for Eddie's story of faith and triumph over adversity. Passing the Test of Faith demonstrates how to lean on God through everything, even when he doesn't answer our prayers the way we would like him to.

1 Thessalonians 5:18 tells us to give thanks in all things. In this book, we are shown exactly how to accomplish this. What an encouraging message Passing the Test of Faith has for Christians, whether new believers or mature in the faith.

– Cynthia Tucker,
Founder of Route 66 Ministries

I am so happy to commend Eddie Johnson's very compelling narrative of his faith journey. This book will encourage many folks to allow life's challenges to be "wind under their wings," moving them ever closer to God!

– Charles Buffington,
Co-Author, *He Said It! I did It!*

Eddie has a poignant story and touching message. Passing the Test of Faith brings one to seek God's reminder of the mustard seed. With growing faith from this little seed in our heart, we can reach oneness with God and fulfillment in life beyond our greatest dreams! Reading this book reminds me of a verse I often rely on, Proverbs 3:5, Trust the Lord with all your heart, and lean not on your own understanding (KJV).

– **Brian Olson,**
Founder and Owner, Café Intermezzo

Faith is never losing hope in the midst of our circumstances, even when there is no glimmer of evidence that we can make it. In these instances, our faith wavers, but because of God, we can always have hope. This isn't easy by any stretch of the imagination. In Passing the Test of Faith, Eddie Johnson helps us understand this. Through his vulnerability and intellect, Eddie produces a real-life picture of what all of our lives resemble. As you read this powerful book of faith, you will see what God made possible for Eddie and be encouraged to know God will do the same for you as your faith mixes with your struggles.

– **Paul Thibodeaux,**
Associate Pastor Impact Church

PASSING THE TEST OF FAITH

The Rewards for Trusting God and Three Fundamental Steps for Walking Through Trials, Adversities, and Hardships

Complimentary Readers Copy

EDDIE L. JOHNSON

ISBN: 978-1-944878-84-9

Scripture quotations taken from the following versions of the Bible: The English Standard Version (ESV), the Good News Translation (GNT), the King James Version (KJV), The Message (MSG), the New International Reader's Version (NIRV), the New International Version (NIV), and the New Living Translation (NLT).

Book design by JETLAUNCH.net

LCCN: 2018900411

This book is dedicated to my mother, Beneva, and son Kendall; you initiated and deepened my intimate relationship with God, opened my eyes to the power of faith, and inspired the lessons for me to share in this book.

CONTENTS

PRAYER OF ACCEPTANCE

Father God, it is with a humble heart that I come before you just to say thank you. I could say it a million times, and it still would not be enough. You have always been there for me in the most troubling and exciting moments of my life.

You showed yourself in my life from the moment I was born, when the doctors told my mother that I might never walk or talk. You proved yourself again when I could not defend myself from being inappropriately touched as a child. Even when I wanted to quit college, you helped me get through so that I could be the first male in my family to graduate with a four-year degree.

Lord, as I fast-forwarded to being an adult, your presence was felt in every weeping moment from the time your angel Kendall was diagnosed with an inoperable brain tumor. Lord, right now my heart is very heavy with emotions of gratitude because, in spite of myself, you promised never to leave or forsake me, and you have more than kept your promise.

Several years ago, when you placed this book assignment on my heart and told me to tell my faith story, I felt a burning inside that never stopped, and I did not know what to believe. I continued to ask you several questions. Who am I to talk about such a powerful word as faith? What will I write? How long should the book be? Would anyone read it or want to hear my story?

Lord, although these were valid concerns, I know the power of obeying you. As I start this book today, on May 29, 2012, I admit I am a little fearful and not sure I am equipped or worthy of this assignment. However, as I pray to you right now, the fear is starting to ease. I know this is not about me, but about you who live within me, where the burning in my heart is coming from.

So right now, Lord, I am stepping out of my comfort zone and putting my fear aside. You once again are challenging me to use my faith, and this requires me to trust you and what I cannot see. Lord, I cannot see how you plan to use me to write this book, how long this book will be, or those whom this book will touch.

Lord, you know I have never been a good writer or reader, so my prayer now is that you will pour into me everything I need, according to your plan, so that through this book, others will be able to experience the joy that comes with exercising their faith in you.

All these things I ask in Jesus' name. Amen!

FOREWORD

In the fall of 1989, on the campus of Florida State University, I had the opportunity to meet Eddie L. Johnson. There a friendship began that led to us being roommates in college, and today our families remain close.

Since that time, I have witnessed Eddie persevere through some "mountain highs and valley lows." Aside from being a friend, I am by vocation a trained Pastor and a trained Social Worker/Counselor. I have spoken with many people who encountered challenges similar to those Eddie has faced. However, despite all he has been through, there is one thing that stands out about Eddie—he has never lost his faith. Therefore, it comes as no surprise that he would write about his faith journey, which is something that he lives daily.

In *Passing the Test of Faith*, Eddie allows us an opportunity to eavesdrop into his life. Holding back nothing, he divulges the innermost pains that he experienced through the many trials, adversities, and hardships of his past.

In this book, Eddie consistently bears witness and testifies that GOD was the common denominator that kept and sustained him in the face of his mountains. Eddie masterfully paints a picture of what having a relationship with and trusting God looks like, and provides three fundamental steps for overcoming those things that can test our faith at any time.

Are you or a loved one dealing with health issues, facing a divorce, feeling anxiety from receiving your pink slip after many years of dedication on the job, or having difficulty relating to your child? Then this is your guide to overcoming your struggles. If you are ready to give up on life, prepare to make a U-turn and move toward God; a power greater than your current situation.

Passing the Test of Faith will encourage you to have the right attitude in difficult situations. It will inspire you to rejoice in God getting the glory after you have transitioned from trial to triumph and motivate you to look for the blessing even in the midst of troubling times. This book will challenge a broken heart to be healed again.

It is my prayer that this book will bless you as much as it has blessed me. This powerful publication is a must read!

Thank you, Eddie, for sharing your testimony.

Reverend Eddy Moise, Jr., M.S.W., M. Div.
Senior Pastor of Bethel AME Church,
Pompano Beach, FL

CROSSING MOUNTAINS

Blessed is the person who keeps on going when times are hard. After they have come through hard times, this person will receive a crown. The crown is life itself. The Lord has promised it to those who love him.

– James 1:12 (NIRV)

In 2003, my son Kendall was diagnosed with an inoperable brain tumor. As a result of his diagnosis, I faced what I call my biggest faith test, which began the journey for this book. As you can imagine, everything in me was being challenged, but nothing was more challenging than the faith I would need to pass the test.

To my surprise, an injury to my left thumb in a ninth-grade basketball game prepared me for this challenge. An injury which I felt for years cost me a promising dream to play basketball in college and maybe professionally.

Through reflection, I came to realize that this injury in 1986, and the events surrounding it, was the beginning of my growing spiritual maturity in faith, the foundation I would build my life on.

I have had many more painful and often overwhelming experiences: family hurt, career challenges, disappointments from others, relationship issues, and grief. I slowed down long enough to look over my life, and I mentally began the process of reviewing these experiences. I called these my "mountain experiences," the trials, adversities, and hardships we all confront in life. To cross my mountains, I had to rely on my faith.

As I moved from mountain to mountain, I saw how God had molded me through my pain and life experiences and blessed me to overcome these life-altering experiences that would have taken most people out. However, God kept me. Not only did He keep me and walk with me through every challenge. He also allowed each one to make me stronger and wiser. With each experience, I was able to offer Him the glory He so richly deserves.

My first mountain was that ninth-grade injury – my very first faith experience that became the foundation of my faith. Now if you are like me, you have memories of playing fun games from your childhood like red light/green light, hopscotch, hide-and-go-seek, jackstones, marbles, or football in the street. You may not remember any life-changing experiences from your younger days. In my case, I was given a test I will never forget, one that I passed by immersing myself in reading Scriptures on faith, ongoing prayer, and an unfailing trust that God had my back.

As if it was yesterday, I remember my mother saying, "Life challenges will always come, and many of them will be tests." For me, taking a test has never been fun, causing me extreme anxiety all the way through college at Florida State University. The only good thing I could say about tests was that they have a beginning and an end, and I could not wait to get to the end.

I did not pass all my "life" tests the first time, and there were many tests I had to retake. Just the thought of retaking a test was painful, especially if the test was long. I was determined to pass the test the first time so the celebration of completion could begin.

Just like the tests we take in the classroom, life will present you with tests that can wear you down. It is imperative that you pass them, or you will have to take those tests again until you get it right. Who wants to be in a perpetual state of test-taking?

While crossing back over the mountain experiences of my past, I started to notice three fundamental steps that proved helpful for moving these mountains and passing my test, so that God could get the glory. These steps were starting with the right attitude, walking with patience, and hearing God's voice.

The book of James outlines these steps for taking life's tests.

My brothers and sisters, you will face all kinds of trouble. When you do, think of it as pure joy. Your faith will be tested. You know that when this happens, it will produce in you the strength (patience) to continue. And you must allow this strength (patience) to finish its work. Then you will be all you should be (mature and complete). You will have everything you need. If any of you needs wisdom, you should ask God for it. He will give it to you. God gives freely to everyone and doesn't find fault. But when you ask, you must believe. You must not doubt. That's because a person who doubts is like a wave of the sea. The wind blows and tosses them around.

– James 1:2-6 (NIRV)

I have found this wisdom from the book of James to be true. As we follow it, we start to develop a sense of peace that can help us prepare, study, assess, and pass any test, no matter how difficult it may be. As believers in Christ, we all have a story of God's goodness and grace in our lives. As we grow in our Christian walk, we recognize God's hand upon us and operating within us. As we follow the steps in James, we learn to pass any test with flying colors and even think of it as joy. For my greatest joy in life is when I am in relationship with God, honoring His will, and accepting His promises.

Even non-believers, once they choose to believe, will have a story to tell, and they too will start the process of learning what it means to have God's guiding hand in their lives.

As I began to recognize God's hand at work in my life, I also realized that He placed a burning desire inside of me to share with others the goodness He has given me. This burning desire has recently helped me discover my purpose, which is "to inspire, encourage, and motivate others to win life challenges, using my faith lessons as a guide."

In writing this book, it is my prayer that everyone who reads it will be inspired to fall in love with God as they build a closer and stronger intimate relationship with Him. I pray that they will be encouraged and strengthened in their trust in God and that through their faith they will be motivated to climb any mountain before them, big or small. I also pray that everyone will be able to experience this feeling of being overwhelmed with God's rewards, but more importantly, GOD'S LOVE: the solution to passing the test!

Join me on this journey through my testimony and the tests that appeared to take me out but instead were designed to strengthen me in my faith. Allow my words and experiences to serve as a cheat sheet that will aid you in your tests. I know that God will help you to overcome your tests of faith just as He did for me.

CHAPTER 1

MY BIGGEST FAITH TEST

*"The greater your knowledge of the goodness and grace
of God on your life, the more likely you are to praise
Him in the storm."*

— Matt Chandler

On May 29, 2000, a day after my thirtieth birthday, God blessed my wife at the time, Treza, and me with a beautiful little boy we named Kendall Alexander Johnson. Since Kendall was our first child, we were very excited, and it showed by the attention we gave him. From birth, Kendall had a great spirit and was a blessing to everyone who met him. He had a way of brightening your day with his infectious smile and caring heart.

One day, I remember we were meeting our pastor for dinner, and Kendall continued to offer him his fries until they were all gone. Our pastor commented that he never saw a boy his age with such a willingness to give. This was no surprise to us because that was something we enjoyed doing as well. Oh, how blessed we were to be Kendall's parents!

Kendall not only blessed others but was also entertaining, especially with his funny use of words and clever way of attempting to be the perfect angel. Anytime Kendall got into trouble, he often turned toward me with a smirk on his face and said, "Daddy did it."

When Kendall was two, from time to time, he showed signs of being startled while asleep, and he began to complain of headaches. Since I suffer from what is called cluster headaches, his pediatrician felt it could be hereditary, and Kendall could be suffering from the same. The doctor ordered a sleep study to see if Kendall's movements were due to something that would explain his headaches.

On July 17, 2003, Treza and I decided to have a family day, and we took off from work to take Kendall to Six Flags Over Georgia. We had an awesome time and even considered purchasing an annual pass so we could experience the excitement over and over again.

Two days later, our lives changed forever.

When I got home from work that evening, Treza told me that Kendall had a bad day at school. His teachers told her he was spitting so much that his shirt was soaked. When I called Kendall over for a hug, I noticed that he could not stand up straight, and he could not take more than five steps without losing his balance. This concerned Treza and me, and we decided to take him to the emergency room.

By the time we arrived at the ER, Kendall was not able to take two steps without losing his balance. We knew then something was wrong. We hoped it was an awful migraine causing the problems and that everything would be okay. A CT scan revealed a much more serious problem.

When the doctor walked into the room, the look on his face said it was a life or death problem. He told us Kendall had a tumor called diffuse intrinsic brainstem glioma. Because the tumor was growing inside his brainstem, it was inoperable.

"Dad, this is very serious," the doctor said, "and we have to hit a home run the first time with radiation and chemotherapy. The only thing that can help this situation is prayer."

As I sat there holding Treza's hand and rubbing Kendall's back, I told the doctor I understood. I turned to Treza while the doctor was still in the room and told her that we were not going to trust in anything but God regarding the news we had just received. I then went silently into prayer. After that, I heard nothing anyone had to say because on the inside I was calling on Jesus for strength, direction, understanding, and comfort. The news was too much for me, and I knew that if I was going to be the father and husband that God called me to be, I needed to have God on one side and Jesus on the other.

I left the room and went outside to find a quiet place to talk to God and to let Him know that no matter what, I was going to have faith in Him. That was hard to do because, naturally, I wanted to fix it myself. Even though it was around 2 a.m., I started calling my prayer warriors – my mother, father, pastor, close friends, and family – to ask everyone to be on their knees and not cease in their prayers for healing and a miracle. I have always heard that there was power in prayer, and I can honestly say that I felt those prayers from my prayer warriors.

Our visit to the hospital during that time lasted for about a week.

The encouragement was amazing. A fraternity brother named Jwyanza left me a message. "Eddie, regardless of what you hear," he said, "there is only one thing you need to trust, and that's God. So you need to keep your faith in Him."

Eddy was a college roommate and one of my best friends who had recently moved to Atlanta from Florida to attend seminary. Eddy continually reminded me to stay faithful and not waiver in what I knew God could do.

The Daniels, who lived across the street, and the Bradfords, who lived around the corner, held prayer vigils with us for healing. They still play a significant part in our journey to this day. The conversations with my pastor, Rev. Johnson, and fraternity brother Ernest helped me to stay focused on the big picture, which was God.

The calls, conversations, and prayers with my mother and father helped keep me focused on my family. They encouraged me to continue looking toward heaven for my strength.

I recall how thankful and blessed we were that we did not have to leave our community of friends to find a good hospital like so many families do. We met so many families who were hours away from their homes and had no one to visit them. We were also blessed to be able to receive emotional support from the Pediatric Brain Tumor Foundation (PBTF). PBTF helps families with emotional support and emergency financial assistance so they can focus on their children diagnosed with a brain tumor. I would eventually serve on the PBTF board for eight years.

Kendall went through chemotherapy and radiation treatments several times a week for several weeks. It was draining on him as well as Treza and me. However, Kendall never lost his winning personality. When he woke up in the recovery room after every radiation treatment, it was exciting for the nurses because he always asked for chips and a "red 'coka' soda," which was his version of saying coke. Because of his clever way of using words, the nurses purchased a case of potato chips and his "red 'coka' soda" to take home after his last treatment.

Kendall always had a smile on his face. Even when the steroids caused him to gain weight and his face to swell, he continued to smile. I remember seeing him look into a mirror as if wondering who he was.

For months after Kendall was diagnosed, I did a lot of praying and reading, looking for God to provide answers. I just did not understand why Kendall had to experience this, and I was confused.

We are good people; we give to others. So why our family? Is it possible that I committed a sin and this was my punishment?

I even wondered at times if I was not a good father and caused this to happen. Was it possible that I was putting work and friends before my family? Nevertheless, the only thing I knew I could do to help Kendall was to rely on my faith.

One day as I was reading through the Bible, I was led to the book of James. Right there in chapter 1, it says, "Count it all joy." I thought to myself, *How can I find joy in this?* As I continued to read down to the twelfth verse, I read that God rewards those who have faith. Well, I was relying on my faith, and the only reward I desired to receive was for Kendall to be healed.

Another day, I read in the book of Mark the story of a boy who was possessed by an evil spirit, which the disciples were trying to cast out. Jesus cast out the evil spirit, but only after the father acknowledged that he did believe, but needed help with his unbelief. Several days later, I reread the story in the book of Luke; my cousin Joslyn called to share a story she also read in the book of Mark. It was the story about the boy from whom Jesus cast out the evil spirit. Hearing this story again from my cousin further confirmed for me that I needed to remain faithful regarding Kendall's illness and his healing.

As the months went on, we continued with treatments and regular visits to Kendall's doctors. Kendall's tumor was not growing, which gave us hope that he was getting better and that it would just take time.

Still relying on my faith during the months to follow, my emotions overwhelmed me at times and I would break down. I just wanted to fix it and make it go away. What father wouldn't? I kept having moments of confusion; I couldn't help but wonder why this was happening to Kendall and our family. We hear about adults with cancer, but never children. So I asked again – why is this happening at my address?

What I did not realize at the time was that God was speaking to me, and in a manner I had not known Him to speak before. It seemed as if every time I had an overwhelming moment, God would speak to me through a gospel song. The first couple of times this happened, I did not realize what was going on. However, I started to notice that whenever my heart was heavy, and I was in my car, the song "The Battle Is the Lord's" by Yolanda Adams would play on the radio. During my most vulnerable times, I would hear this song, as if God was reminding me that this was not my battle; it was His battle. Once I realized this was God's way of talking to me, I started listening very intently to the words. I will never forget what I felt then and still do to this day when I hear this song. Each time, it reminds me that the battle, whatever it is, belongs to God; that all things work according to God's plan and will; and He wants to use me for His glory.

Since 2003, this song has given me the comfort and assurance I needed to turn all my painful experiences over to God. I find it very interesting that, even today, this song comes on when I am dealing with my hardest situations in life.

Two of my most memorable moments during Kendall's illness came in December 2003, five months after his diagnosis. The first one was when Treza's parents, aunt, and uncle came for the holidays. As we gathered around the table for Christmas dinner, I announced that I was about to bless the food. Kendall stopped me and said, "Let me do it! Let me bless the food!" This surprised us all, and I allowed him to bless our Christmas dinner. He said the Lord's Prayer from beginning to end, with everyone repeating him verse by verse. I realized Kendall had learned to recite the Lord's Prayer on his own by repeating it after me every morning on our way to his school, something I did not know he could do. What was more important to me is that Kendall knew how to pray, and that helped me realize he had his own relationship with God.

The second most memorable moment was when we found out that we were expecting another child. At first, this was very hard for me to accept, and I remember having a few choice words with God, saying, "If you're trying to prepare me for a replacement, that's not what I want. I want Kendall to be healed." I even went as far as not praying for about two days, thinking that God did not care about what my family was experiencing. After being rebellious for several days, I realized I needed to continue to trust God no matter what.

Around that time, we shared with Kendall that he was going to be a big brother. We showed him a picture of the sonogram, and when he looked at it, he said, "I don't see no baby." I told him it was in his mommy's tummy. He said, "Let me see," and preceded to rub her stomach.

That night, he fell asleep with the sonogram picture in his hand. Kendall was a bit spoiled and very much loved, so he slept in the bed with us every night of his life, except for the one night that we attempted to try and get him to sleep in his bed. We did not realize then that we had an angel sleeping with us every day. After he was asleep, I took the picture out of his hand and placed it on the nightstand.

When Kendall woke up the next morning, he said, "Hey! Where is the picture of my baby? That's my picture and my baby." Then I asked him, "Hey buddy, what do you want, a boy or girl?" He said, "I want two babies," and I replied, "There's not two, there's only one." He responded, "I want two babies," and ran off to another room. For about a month, Kendall would say, "I want two babies" each time he was asked. Then he finally said, "I want a girl baby."

As the months went on, we continued the weekly checkups and bi-monthly scans. His condition remained consistent until the beginning of April, when Kendall's scan revealed that his tumor had grown.

By this time, Kendall had lost his ability to speak and the ability to walk on his own. He was starting to lose his sight because the tumor was on his brain stem. After receiving the results from the April scan, we were presented with options for two new treatments available for this type of tumor. We could have gone to St. Jude Children's Research Hospital in Memphis for treatment, or we could stay at Scottish Rite Children's Hospital in Atlanta. We decided through prayer to remain at Scottish Rite for the new treatment they had just received.

Kendall was admitted to the hospital for the first time since his diagnosis. Many friends and members of our church came to visit and pray with us. Because of our faith, many of the nurses asked if they could join us when we prayed as a group.

A week later, Kendall grew very weak, and he was not doing well at all. On the morning of April 28, 2004, Kendall passed away in the hospital. This was the hardest moment of my life and the most gut-wrenching feeling I ever felt.

During the planning of Kendall's homegoing service, I told Rev. Johnson, my pastor, that I wanted to speak.

"Are you sure you want to do this?" he asked me. "It will not be easy."

I told him I would be okay, and I could do it.

On the morning of the service, I went to Kendall's room and sat on his bed to gather my thoughts. There God granted me the peace I needed; it was the peace that surpasses all understanding.

"Peace is what I leave with you; it is my own peace that I give you. I do not give it as the world does. Do not be worried and upset; do not be afraid."
– John 14:27 (GNT)

At Kendall's service, I had the opportunity to address everyone who came to say their goodbyes and support Treza and me. I shared how I was the proudest father ever, and I knew what it must feel like to have your son drafted as the number one draft pick for a professional sports team. I shared this with everyone because, during the nine months after Kendall's diagnosis, he touched and changed the hearts of many people. We know this because of the stories they shared. For example, one young lady shared that she had never prayed on her knees, however because of Kendall, she started getting on her knees before praying.

As I was walking to the car after the service, a gentleman from the communications ministry at our church came over to express that out of all the homegoing services he attended; this was the most uplifting service he had ever seen. "I have never seen someone with the strength you have," he said. "Never stop keeping your faith."

As I sat in the car, about to leave the church, the husband of a well-known person in Atlanta, a gentleman I had never met before, asked if he could speak to me. "The only thing I would like to say to you is thank you," he said. "You will probably never know why, but you were a blessing to my family and me today."

I learned that a fraternity brother leaving the service expressed to others that he needed to make a change for his wife and kids.

As a father, hearing these things made me feel good and reminded me that *Kendall's short life blessed many people, and he served his purpose.*

I have said that if God gave me a choice, I would have chosen to let Kendall go because it would have been selfish of me to stop him from getting to the place we all hope to one day get to ourselves. We have to do our part and make sure our lives are right if we want to see Kendall again. I know when I arrive the first person to meet me at heaven's door will be Kendall, and he will probably say, "Hey, what took you so long?"

Exactly one week after Kendall passed, Treza and I found out that we were having a "girl baby," which was exactly what Kendall wanted. I remember saying to myself, "Kendall must have known he was going to get his girl baby."

Four months later, we were blessed with a daughter, whom we named Kennedy. As you can imagine, when Kennedy was born we were filled with great joy, and we showered her with love. As I reflect back to that moment when I disagreed with God, I now realize, as always, that God knew what He was doing, and He just needed me to get on His program of acceptance.

Our neighbor, Sylvia, watched Kennedy for seven months, and then we decided it was time to put her into daycare. We then found out that we were expecting again! This came as a huge surprise because we were still grieving the departure of Kendall and enjoying a newborn. Now we were looking for daycare for two children.

As Treza and I visited various centers, I started to feel overwhelmed. Daycare in our area was extremely expensive for two children, ranging from $1,800 to $2,300 a month. I did not say too much out loud, but inside I was praying and asking, "Lord, how are we going to do this?"

Shortly after praying, I remember sitting at the intersection of McGinnis Ferry Road and Highway 141, where I heard God's voice say, "If I blessed you with them, I will give you everything you need to take care of them." At that moment, I again received the peace I felt the day of Kendall's homegoing service. I then knew we would have the money to take care of every expense.

The very next daycare we visited would only do tours on certain days, but they allowed us to peek into the room where Kennedy would be. As Treza and I walked back to our car, we heard a young lady calling, "Eddie and Treza, Eddie and Treza!" When we turned around, we saw Kendall's favorite teacher, Karen, from his daycare center. She was now working at this one! Karen came running to hug us. We saw Karen's presence as a blessing, and as you can imagine, this was the daycare we selected.

Three days later, I was traveling on business to Augusta, Georgia, and Treza went for an ultrasound. After her visit, she called me laughing and crying. I asked, "What is wrong? What is wrong?"

"You're not going to believe this," she said.

"Believe what?"

She said the nurse asked her, "How would you feel if you had two babies?"

"Yes, I know," I replied. "We have Kennedy and a new baby on the way."

"No," Treza said. "We're having twins!"

I was speechless.

Treza went on to say that the nurse used the same words as Kendall did when she said "two babies."

My first thought was, "Wait one minute, God! You gave me peace with two children, not three, and $1,800 to $2,300 for daycare, not $2,700 to $3,450."

I called Rev. Johnson to share the news with him. I told him that, of course, I was not the Biblical figure Job, but felt I was having a Job-like experience. Job lost his children, but he was blessed with more. I lost Kendall, and I would be blessed with more. Rev. Johnson said that even though I was not Job, I showed faith like Job, and God blesses those who have faith.

At the beginning of 2006, God blessed me, Treza, and Kennedy with twin boys, Christian and Cameron.

CHAPTER 2

OVERCOMING WITH FAITH

The key to our relationship with God is in our faith.
– Eddie Johnson

"In this world, nothing can be said to be certain except death and taxes," Benjamin Franklin wrote in 1789.

I would like to add one additional certainty of life: "Your faith will be tested." None of us is exempt from a faith test, and at some point in our lives, we will have to take one. Everyone who has walked this earth has had their faith tested.

Growing up, we heard many stories of those who demonstrated faith, including Noah, David, and Moses, to name a few. However, best known for his test of faith is Job.

Job – a man who was God-fearing, honest, wealthy, and who avoided evil doings – found himself in a faith test he did not see coming. With God's permission, Satan tested Job's faithfulness. Satan believed that Job was only faithful because God had blessed him with everything one could think of having. God, knowing this was not the case, allowed Satan to have power over everything that Job owned. However, God gave Satan one condition, and that was not to kill Job (Job 2:6). Great suffering came upon Job, causing him to lose just about everything: his ten children, his livestock, and his servants. His wife suggested he should curse God and die. But Job continued to worship God. Even after losing everything, he exemplified true faithfulness, and God blessed him with twice as much as he had before.

Questions for Reflection:

Has your faith ever been tested? Have you ever doubted, worried, or feared something?

> **Faith is trusting God to do something, believing His will is best, while our eyes are blind to what He will do.**

To bring meaning to faith, we often refer to Hebrews 11, which is considered the faith chapter. The first verse of this chapter is the Scripture we are familiar with: *Now faith is the substance of things hoped for, the evidence of things not seen* (Hebrews 11:1 – KJV). In other words, faith is trusting God to do something, believing His will is best, while our eyes are blind to what He will do. The reward of faith is to receive God's promise according to His will for our life. It is important that we acknowledge the word "hope" in this Scripture. Notice that it does not say "wished for," because a wish is what we want. On the other hand, to have hope is to expect God to do something. Many of us find this a hard submission of self because we have to wait in expectation according to God's will and timing.

A good example of the reward for having faith can be found in Romans 4:13-25, where we find the reward of Abraham's blind faith. In the original story found in Genesis 17:1-5, God promises Abraham that he will make him the father of many nations. Even at the age of 99 and knowing that his wife Sarah was too old to have children, Abraham did not second-guess God's promise. Abraham did not let his aging body keep him from believing and having hope in what God said he would do. God's promise did not come to Abraham because he was a good man. He received the promise of God because of his faith, which made him right with God.

Even when our eyes cannot see a reason to expect God to do something, we can still trust God's power and will. It is through our faith that we can position ourselves to receive what God has for us, knowing He always wants us to receive His best.

Expressions of Faith

Here are ways I have seen faith expressed over the years:

- *Now faith is being sure of what we hope for and certain of what we do not see* (Hebrews 11:1 – NIRV).
- Faith is seeing the light with your heart when all your eyes see is darkness ahead. - Barbara Johnson
- Faith is what you believe God will bring to pass. - Anonymous
- Faith is daring the soul to go beyond what the eyes can see. - William Newton Clark

- Faith is a living, daring confidence in God's grace, so sure and certain that a man could stake his life on it a thousand times. – Martin Luther King, Jr.
- Faith is trusting God to do something, believing His will is best, while our eyes are blind to what He will do. - Eddie Johnson

Question for Reflection:

In your own words, how would you express faith?

The Mountain Experience

"Because you have so little faith. Truly I tell you, if you have faith as small as a mustard seed, you can say to this mountain, 'Move from here to there,' and it will move. Nothing will be impossible for you."

– Matthew 17:20 (NIV)

I do not know about you, but I cannot visualize moving a mountain – a big rock that we think of and often see. It is just too overwhelming to imagine. Instead, the mountain I visualize is the problem standing before us, which we can refer to as trials, adversities, and hardships. Some of these mountains are small, some large, and if you allow it, some can consume you. Some of these mountains are small, some large, and if you allow it, some can consume you.

The blessing we have, as found in this verse from the book of Matthew, is that our mustard-seed faith does not need to be nearly as big as our mountain. We just need to allow our mustard-seed-sized faith to be activated, knowing that, by faith, mountains can be moved.

Mountain experiences look like really big problems. *Consider: Is an amicable divorce possible when kids are involved? Can the body really heal from what a doctor says is a fatal illness? How about digging out of a mountain of debt? You can move these mountains – I've seen it done! You guessed it: faith is your superpower that moves them.*

During this mountain-moving process – a test of faith – we often experience the revealing of God's reward and His favor for our lives, both of which are great! Moreover, there is an unanticipated bonus. During a mountain experience, we build a stronger relationship with God and have the opportunity to be a witness for God to others.

Regardless of how big the mountain is, we can use certain fundamental steps so that we can witness it being moved for the glory of God and for our good. These steps are starting with the right attitude, walking with patience, and hearing God's voice. They help us move mountains and get us through the trials so we can reap the reward(s) God has promised through our faith.

Imagine with me for a moment, you are driving down the road and from a distance, God allows you to see a mountain ahead, representing your trials, adversities, and hardships. This mountain may be sickness, finances, career, or relationships. The mountain may be one, two, five, or even ten years away. From a distance, this mountain does not look insurmountable, and it is something you feel you can deal with when you get there. However, once you finally reach the mountain and are standing at its base, you quickly realize you need to deal with issues and challenges that you could not see from a distance.

When we come up against a mountain, we seek ways to get to the other side of it. The best method I have found for dealing with our mountains is practicing our faith, allowing God to guide our steps. I don't recommend we try to take the route on our own, thinking, for example, that just walking around the base will be a short and easy path. Sometimes we have to climb that mountain – not just walk around it. You see, taking the short and easy way may put us ahead of God and His time for our arrival, and we may bypass the reward. Missing the reward may very well put us back where we started, and then we will have to start over.

If it is God's will that we climb the mountain, we must use our faith first, tracking God down for His navigation system. Aligning our way to God puts us on a path that strengthens and improves our relationship with Him while on the journey.

Our Faith Mountains Have Purpose

Every mountain is designed to bring us closer to God, allowing us to have a more intimate relationship with Him. Mountains can have various purposes, and many times we may not know what the purpose is until later in the journey.

For example, the purpose of your mountain might be to stop you from achieving the rewards and blessings God has for you. Know this: the devil does not want you to receive the blessings that are stored up for you.

The mountain may also be placed there to test the strength of your faith. Until you are facing your mountain head-on, you may never know how strong your faith is.

Another mountain purpose I will share might surprise you. The mountain may not be for you, but for someone else to be blessed through your experience. God knows whom He can use to fulfill His purpose and

His will. This type of mountain experience can be very painful, but when you realize how God was protecting you through your journey, and how it blessed someone else by bringing them closer to Him, your pain will instantly turn into overwhelming joy.

I would have never believed this until I experienced it for myself.

I had a new manager at work who tried everything possible to take me out of the game. I experienced bad performance reviews, lost compensation even when goals were met, unnecessary pressure to get me to leave the company, and lack of respect as a person.

Two days before the start of my problems with the manager, God, through prayer and meditation, spoke to my spirit to let me know that He would cover and prepare me for the storm ahead. I did not know that the storm would last for more than three years.

I will never forget the day I received a call that the manager had resigned. I instantly thanked God for the blessing of His covering and that the games were now over. That evening as I left my office for Vacation Bible School, I was so eager to tell someone the exciting news! I tried calling my mother, my cousin Lavetta, my best friend Gene, and my mentor Vinnie. But I could not reach any of them to share my excitement.

Little did I know that those missed calls would be a set-up for a blessing to come later.

The lesson at Vacation Bible School was "Being Happy When You Have Every Reason to Be Unhappy." As our pastor ended the lesson, I was spiritually led to get up from my seat and share with my pastor how being happy in the storm turned into a blessing.

As everyone else approached the altar for prayer, our pastor called me up to share my testimony. I was so grateful to share how I got through the three years. As I went back to the alter I stood next to a church member named Edward and grabbed his hand. He hugged me and said, "I am going through the same thing right now, and that was the purpose of me needing prayer." His struggle had just started in the last month, and this was the hope he needed to continue to stay faithful and to do so with a happy spirit.

I grabbed the right hand of the lady standing on my other side, and she said she was going through the same thing and needed to hear my testimony. This renewed her strength to continue to trust God also. As I left the church, several others said they were experiencing something similar and that to hear someone receive victory was a blessing for them.

I then realized there was a reason I could not reach any of the four people I tried to call as I left the office. There was no doubt in my mind that God silenced the ring of those phones so I could share the blessings at church for someone who needed to hear it most. My mountain experience was also for the others I encountered that night. My faith was not only hope and inspiration but a light to others who needed to see it.

> Faith is so awesome because it is like a good movie where you never know how it will end. God has a way of making the ending better than the beginning.

Apparently, it was also for my manager, who gave me a hard time, which tested my faith. Before leaving, he apologized for getting off on a wrong foot with me. He said that he had learned several things while watching me from afar, including that spending more time with his family and being a better parent to his children was more important than chasing a career.

Trusting God While on Our Faith Journey

"Ask, and it will be given to you. Search, and you will find. Knock, and the door will be opened to you. Everyone who asks will receive. The one who searches will find. The door will be opened to the one who knocks."
– **Matthew 7:7-8 (NIRV)**

To have faith, you must trust that God can do it and believe that He will. So many struggle with this because they do not get the answers or results they want fast enough.

Yes, God wants us to ask Him for anything, and He encourages us to do so. However, we must understand that God wants the best for us and will provide it according to His will and the perfect plan He has for our lives. This is not always easy, especially when we think we know what is best for ourselves at that moment.

It is critical to understand that when we go to God, we may not get what we want. If this happens, we should remember that His will is far better than ours. I gained a better appreciation of this through my years as a Christian as I got closer to God, realizing one of His many attributes is omniscience. Omniscience means God is all-knowing about my past, present, and future, and because of His all-knowing power, He knows what's best for me. Once we completely understand and accept this, our faith grows, because we then recognize God's love, His strength, His power, and His protection for us.

Question for Reflection:

How many mountains has your faith moved? In other words, what have you trusted God to do that was too hard for you to handle?

Finding the Blessings While on Our Faith Journey

As a new or experienced Christian, our faith will not grow by just merely saying the word "faith." That would be too easy. Faith grows under the pressure of mountains of trials, adversities, and hardships. When these mountains appear, don't give in or think God is punishing you, because He is not. The mountain is there to help you grow your trust in Him while blessing you throughout the journey. Finding the blessings while in the middle of a mountain experience can be tricky for most of us because our focus is usually on the problem we are facing. However, it is one of the greatest feelings you will ever experience.

I have always known that you could find the blessing while in the storm, but I don't think I truly embraced and understood it until I lost my job.

In April 2017, I celebrated twenty years of service with the company I went to work for after graduating from Florida State University. This company and the many great people I worked with were a blessing to me. But that month, I was included in a significant staff reduction.

Now, most people would find being downsized after twenty years to be tragic, but I was able to find several blessings in unemployment.

The first blessing was that it allowed me the opportunity to go on my first mission trip outside of the country, which turned out to be humbling and a rewarding blessing. To see people living with far less than we have but who have so much love, joy, passion, and faith was a blessing to witness.

The second blessing was that it allowed me to spend more time with God, building my relationship with Him. I have enjoyed quiet time reflecting on Him and the many things He has done for me, as well as the things He has revealed and promised to me.

I am most grateful for the additional blessing of having the time and opportunity to finish this book, which God placed on my heart to do more than five years ago.

Ironically, shortly before being released from my job, I had a conversation with one of my well-respected managers who truly has a heart to serve others and is someone for whom I have deep respect. My manager asked me about my children, how they were doing in school, and what activities they were participating in currently. My kids are so important to me, so being asked this always meant a lot.

Before we hung up, my manager said, "Eddie, I have to ask you, how are you coming on your book?"

My response hadn't changed in four years. "I am still working on it," I said. "But with work being so busy and taking care of my kids as a single dad, I just have not been able to find the time I need to work on it. But I am going to finish it! I just have to make the time!"

Little did I know that in six days I would have time to finish the book.

The night before my last day, I had a strong urge to stop what I was doing and go to the Wednesday night service at church. As I drove there, knowing that I might soon be without a job, I started to feel disappointment and hurt, which was causing me to experience anxiousness and worry about how I was going to provide for my kids, and confusion regarding my career and what I would do next.

I received a blessing for being obedient to God's urging that I go to church that night. Submitting to God's urging and being willing to stop what I was doing was probably the best thing I did for the first three months of the year. The Scripture the senior pastor, the Rev. Dr. Michael T. McQueen, shared seemed chosen just for me.

> *Don't worry about anything; instead, pray about everything. Tell God what you need, and thank him for all he has done. Then you will experience God's peace, which exceeds anything we can understand. His peace will guard your hearts and minds as you live in Christ Jesus.*
> — **Philippians 4:6-7 (NLT)**

As tears flowed down my face, I heard God's voice say, "Trust Me and see what I will do. What I am going to do will blow your mind. I just need you to trust me." I found this interesting because my faith requires me to trust God, which I do in all things, and now God was telling me to trust Him even more.

Based on what I knew God had done before, I thought to myself, *What do I have to lose; if there is anyone I can trust, it is God.*

God was letting me know that, once again, this was not about me. This was about Him and the time we would have together. This was also the opportunity to complete the work that He had called me to do, which was to finish this book. Had I not been in relationship with God, it's possible I would have missed what He was telling me about this journey of my life.

It was as though God was sitting next to me, holding my hand, and wiping the tears from my eyes. I instantly experienced the peace that surpasses all understanding. The peace was so great that I remember saying, "God, if you are ready to close a chapter of twenty years with the company I work for, then I am willing so that you can open a new chapter in my life."

The next day I was driving home, and the song "The Battle Is the Lord's" by Yolanda Adams came on the radio. Once again, God was nudging me with this song, just like He did in my biggest faith test. It reminded me that this was not my battle, that all things work according to His plan, and that He wanted to use me for His glory.

Choosing to finish this book and postpone my job search would require me to be radical in my faith. After all, James 2:7 says *...faith by itself, if it is not accompanied by action, is dead* (NIV). I put my faith into action, knowing that God can and will do much with this because I trust Him to do so.

Questions for Reflection:

When was the last time you put your faith into action? What did God do with it?

Displaying Faith for the Blessing of Others

Did you know that God does His best work when we show our faith in Him? Others are watching to see how we are going to handle the test that is before us. When we operate in faith, others have the opportunity to see God, allowing Him to get the glory. After all, that's what this Christian journey is all about. We have to remember that God wants to use His children to operate so that He can shine His light and love through us.

So, what does that mean? We would all like it if God came and sat on top of our mountain and gave directions, telling us what to do to get over it, around it, through it – or even out of it. Instead, God will use our situations so that others watching can see what He can do when we put our trust in Him. If this were not the case, none of us would ever have a testimony of His love for us and how He works. The only testimonies we would be able to share are the stories we have read about in the Bible.

Others who are focused on our Christian journey will be more apt to watch what we *do*, rather than what we *say*, making our faith walk more valuable in the eyes of others than our faith talk. As they see us pushing through the hurt and pain of our trials, they will no doubt wonder how we will pull through it.

The blessing of our faith is displayed when the test and trials are over, and others see the light of the Holy Spirit within us shining, helping them make a decision for Jesus Christ, and helping fellow Christians strengthen their faith. Our walk may be the only walk others see, so it is important that we pass the test. God can use our faith and witness to help transform the hearts and minds of others.

Questions for Reflection:

What event(s) tested your faith?
When did it happen?
How did it feel when the test began and when it ended?
How did God bring you through it?
Were others blessed because of your faith walk?

These are some questions I had to answer for myself, and as you go through this journey, you will find answers to these questions as well if you do not have them already.

Put your faith in action and watch what God does with it.

– Eddie Johnson

CHAPTER 3

MY FIRST FAITH EXPERIENCE

The greatest legacy one can pass on to one's children and grandchildren is not money or other material things accumulated in one's life, but rather a legacy of character and faith.

– Billy Graham

Faith carried me through my biggest test. As others asked about it, I began to wonder how and when my faith began. So I started tracing the path between the mountains I had climbed before Kendall's diagnosis.

Going back over my mountains of trials and tribulations was an interesting process, and each mountain brought back emotions that, at first, I did not want to

recall. However, I realized that each of these mountains was necessary for my spiritual molding. When I
got back to my first faith experience, these emotions
quickly began to fade away and turn into gratitude as
I started to think about how my life had played out. I
started to visualize how I could share my story and help
others through speaking engagements. I even started
thinking that my story would be good for a talk show.
As I got bigger in my thinking, tears rolled down my
face as I began to imagine certain scenes from a movie
about my story.

I share with everyone that I have been blessed, and
it is only because of God's grace and mercy that I have
a story to tell. Even you have a story that you can share,
and there is someone who will be blessed by hearing
your testimony.

I had experienced some difficult moments in life
growing up in Jacksonville, Florida. My mother and
father divorced when I was only four. About the same
time, I experienced being touched inappropriately by a
family member, which affected me until I was able to
forgive the offense later in life. I am so grateful for the
power of forgiveness; it does free you up.

Seeing my mother struggle to raise my sister Lisa
and me as a single parent had its challenging moments.
I would wake up in the middle of the night to hear my
mother crying in prayer. To this day, I have never asked
my mother about those prayers. I can only imagine that
they were for clothes when we needed them, food when
the pantry was empty, and bills to be paid. Those were
some tough times, but I never went hungry, and I always
had clothes to wear.

However, these challenges meant nothing when
it came to the love we had for Chad, a little boy who
lived next door. When my mother learned he needed

a place to live, she couldn't open our front door to him fast enough. Money may have been an issue, but there was always enough to share with this boy. Chad became my brother when he was seven years old and my mother adopted him.

I made some mistakes growing up, making things even more difficult for my mother. She was a strict disciplinarian, and she had no tolerance for misbehavior. "If you go to jail, don't call me because I am not coming to get you," Mom told me and my sister and brother. Our strict upbringing was by far one of the best things my mother could have given us, because none of us ever did anything that required us to spend time in jail. I never wanted to experience her promise to never pick me up from jail, so I always tried to make right decisions.

I came close to testing her one summer when I was around eleven years old. My best friend and I almost went to jail for hanging around the wrong boys. We could easily have been blamed for some thefts and other criminal acts those boys committed. To some degree, we were blessed on that day. Those boys did the right thing by telling the police officers we had nothing to do with the situation for which they were being jailed.

It was less than a blessing when my mother gave me what we called back then a whipping or a beating. I almost wished I had gone to jail, because the whipping seemed never to end!

Even with all her challenges, my mother always found a way to keep us active in church and sports. She said this kept us busy when we weren't in school. We liked going to church, and I enjoyed playing football and basketball, while my sister cheered. I believe my athletic ability came from my dad, who was pretty good at football; he played defensive back in high school and was known as "White Shoes Johnson." (However,

I do not think he played football as well as he can sing, especially, when he is singing for the Lord.)

For many years I enjoyed playing Pop Warner football before being introduced to my favorite sport: basketball. From the time I started playing basketball in the sixth grade, I was pretty good. In fact, I was the star of the team.

By the time I got to the eighth grade at JEB Stuart Junior High School (now called JEB Stuart Middle School), I was fearless. In my mind, no one could beat me – not even the best NBA players at the time. Several days before our first game against our rivalry school, Jeff Davis Junior High School, two of our five starting players got sick. The first game of the season was a big deal, and everyone was saying we were going to lose. Having the mind of an athlete who did not like to lose, I told my teammates that we would not lose the game; we would just have to go out there and play our best, even without two of our starting players.

The gym was packed that evening. Everyone had come to see Stacey, who was the star of our ninth-grade team and eventually became a McDonald's All-American and had a very successful college career. With all the nerves and negative talk going around, my teammates were not ready to play. But I was, and I wanted to win. The game came down to free throws at the very end, and we won the game, 45 to 43, that everyone said we were going to lose! I broke a school record by scoring 41 of the 45 points. After the first game of my eighth-grade year, I realized just how good of an athlete I was and could potentially become. I felt I was on my way to some big things as an athlete and in life.

I also participated in track and field, where I finished fourth place in the county championship meet in the high jump. The winners ahead of me were ninth graders, which assured me I would have a good chance at winning first place the next year. As you can imagine, my eighth-grade year in middle school was awesome for me, but it was nothing like the year that was to come.

I can remember my ninth-grade year like it was yesterday; it was at that time the best year of my life. In addition to playing sports, I also played the trombone in school and sat in first chair, meaning I was the leader of my section. I was voted most outstanding bandsman of the year.

That year, I was the co-captain and quarterback of the football team. Had you seen me warming up on the field, you probably would not have known what position I was going to play. I can joke about it now, but even as a quarterback, I wore braces on both knees to help protect them from injury. I even wore a white neck collar, which you normally see linebackers wearing, but never a quarterback. At the end of the season, I was selected most outstanding "offensive" back. I managed to finish the season without any major injuries so that I could play basketball, which I loved the most.

After such a great basketball year in eighth grade, I was excited to be back indoors on the hardwood court. I was excited because I could dunk the basketball even though I was only in the ninth grade – a rare feat for middle-school ballplayers. If I could do this in a game, I would have the entire school talking; it would make anyone feel as if they were on top of the world. I was the captain of the team and at the end of the season, I was selected the most valuable player of the year.

Even though our team struggled to win games that year, I performed well. During the ninth game against Highlands Junior High School, I got my first dunk of the season. Several coaches felt I could be one of the top players coming out of Jacksonville by my senior year if my level of play continued to improve.

With only three games left in the season, we played our next game at home against Lakeshore Junior High School. I dunked the ball two times in the first half of the game, and I felt like I could jump to the moon.

With less than two minutes left in the game, I made a steal and was headed to make my third dunk. As I dunked the ball, one of the Lakeshore players tried to block me. Instead, he pushed me off balance, causing me to fall. I thought I was going to land face down. I tried to catch myself, but I hit the floor hard, and I mean very hard. The coaches ran onto the court – along with my mother – to see if I was okay.

I grabbed my right knee, which was in much pain. Then I noticed that my left hand was feeling numb. As I looked at it, I could not believe what I saw. My left thumb was bent back to the top of my hand. As you could imagine, it freaked me out.

My mother took me to the emergency room, where the doctor told me I had sprained my right knee, sprained my left wrist, and broke and dislocated my left thumb. I would need to see an orthopedic surgeon. Wow, this was not good timing with our last game a week away.

"I need you to put the thumb back in place," I told the doctor, "because I need to play our last game. I just need you to fix it."

The doctor looked at me and said, "Son, let me put it to you another way. You will not be playing anytime soon, and you will need surgery on your thumb."

Back then we used to play at least one game during school hours, and all the students would be there to watch. Our in-school game was going to be against our rivalry school Jeff Davis, the school I had broken the record against while in the eighth grade. This particular game had been on my mind all season because, in my opinion, I was going to show out, be unstoppable, and if given a chance, dunk the ball on someone and make the gym go wild. Missing the last game of the regular season was devastating.

Two days later, I had surgery on my left thumb. After the surgery, I remember feeling disappointed in myself and thinking all my dreams of being a successful basketball player and athlete were gone.

Following basketball season was track, where I participated in the 880 relay, long jump, and high jump, of course. I had one goal in mind: to win the county championship in the high jump.

However, there were a couple of problems.

First, my doctor advised me not to participate in the high jump for fear that my thumb had not healed yet. If I injured it again, I might lose it. Being determined, I ignored his advice and decided to do the high jump anyway. To protect my thumb from injury during every track practice and meet, my coaches would wrap my hand in a football pad and wrap a sleeping pillow over it. (I wish I had pictures!) This year was much harder after the injury. I struggled just to place in the top at any track meet. It was embarrassing, to say the least, and it seemed as if all my jumps were getting worse with each week that passed.

The second problem I had – probably the most significant of this experience – was that I had lost my confidence and suffered a broken spirit.

I wanted to know what my chance was for winning athlete of the year for the school. Coach Guido, the athletic director and head football coach, shocked me when he said, "You are a good athlete, and we have several of those this year. For you to win athlete of the year, you would need to win in one of the track events during the upcoming district and county championship meets."

To make it to the county championship meet, I would have to finish in the top four from my district, which was one of two school districts in Jacksonville. I thought to myself, *Forget the county championship. How am I going to place at the district meet?* The high jump was my best chance, but I had not won or placed with jumps greater than 5'2 and 5'4 in this event the entire track season. I felt Coach Guido had lost his mind.

Apparently, Coach Guido didn't think it was enough that I was the co-captain and quarterback of the football team, the most outstanding offensive back, the captain of the basketball team, and the most valuable basketball player of the year. I walked away a little perplexed and wondering what else I needed to do.

I realized I had a problem, but I did not know how to fix it. To me, my problem was big, and it was confidence. I learned very early that to be competitive and comfortable with what I was doing in sports, I needed this. Confidence in athletics, which very few had at my age, had come naturally to me, and now the lack of it was about to cost me everything.

My spirit was broken, and I knew I needed to do something different.

One evening I sat down with my mother and shared that I might not win athlete of the year. She had seen my ups and downs as a boy, as an athlete, and as a person who tried to do things right. My mother would go to the basketball court and pass me the ball while I shot free throws and jumpers. Never complaining, she would even get up very early in the morning and drive her car behind me while I ran a couple of miles before school.

As a single mother, she taught me to cook and clean at an early age. She told me I needed to know how to do these things; in the event something ever happened to her, I would know how to take care of my sister, brother, and myself.

But by far the best thing she ever taught me when I was very young was about God. She would always tell me – and still does today – in all things, trust God with all my heart and allow Him to do the rest.

So I sat down with my mother, overcome with emotions because I was not going to win the high jump and this was going to ruin my chance at winning the athlete of the year award. My mother, looking at the tears running down my face, said, *"Son, do you know what faith is?"*

It was at this point my life truly changed forever!

My mother told me that regardless of how hard things may seem, if I trust God and His will, through Him, I can do anything. She said that God has given all of us some level of faith and that over time, our faith grows stronger so we are better prepared for the next test that lies ahead. And then she hit me with the whammy: *It was important that I pass this faith test.*

My mother told me to look at my faith as being on a ninth-grade level and to think about all the grades and tests I had to pass to get here. She told me that all my life God has been giving me tests, which I continued to pass so that I could move on to the next grade in my faith. God was allowing me to be tested now, and it would be pass or fail. If I failed, I would have to retake the test, and maybe even go back a grade level or two. She told me that this was a test that I was capable of passing. I remember thinking, *I do not want to take a chance of going back as far as the seventh grade.*

My mother shared with me several Scriptures on faith, and she encouraged me to read them every day. I do not remember all the Scriptures she gave me, but I do remember these:

- *Now faith is the substance of things hoped for, the evidence of things not seen* (Hebrews 11:1 – KJV)
- *No one can please God without faith, for whoever comes to God must have faith that God exists and rewards those who seek him* (Hebrews 11:6 – GNT)
- *"Because you have so little faith. Truly I tell you, if you have faith as small as a mustard seed, you can say to this mountain, 'Move from here to there,' and it will move. Nothing will be impossible for you."* (Matthew 17:20 – NIV)

I read my faith Scriptures diligently every day for a week. I started feeling excited and confident again. Along with feeling motivated, I began to believe in my heart that if it was God's will, I could jump high enough to win – even the county championship.

A week later, at the district meet, I was having the best meet of my life. Without knocking the bar down once, I cleared 5'4, 5'6, 5'8, 5'10, and 6'0 before failing to clear my jump. After clearing 6'0, it was time to attempt 6'2, the district record set the year before when I finished in fourth place, and I was going for it. As I prepared to take my jump at 6'2, I felt my footing off and jumped out too far from the bar, knocking it down. As the bar fell, I landed on the mat, sliding my right arm across the triangle-shaped bar and cutting it. I should have received stitches. The five-inch scar reminds me of that jump to this day.

This was the third time I had knocked down the bar at the district meet. Even with a bleeding arm, I had my confidence back. I told my opponent Desi, who had knocked the bar down two times, that I would take second place this week, but do not expect me to take second place at the county championship meet.

The championship meet a week later would show-case the top track and field athletes across Jacksonville. The winner would earn all the bragging rights and be considered the best at his event. I continued to read my faith Scriptures every day, believing in my heart that I could jump high enough to win. I prayed that God would allow me to perform as well as I did in the district meet – but better.

The meet started out well, and I was jumping just as well as I did in the district meet, if not better. It came down to Desi and me again for the county championship. We had both cleared 6'0 as we had done at the district meet, and we were now jumping for 6'2. Desi had knocked the bar down two times, and I had only knocked it down one time. As Desi made his first attempt at 6'2, he knocked the bar down for the third time. This allowed me to finish first and win the county championship in the high jump!

Yes, that day I won the championship in the high jump. I also went on to win the athlete of the year award.

What I did not know that day was that *I became a champion of champions.* I became the champion of disappointment, hurt, and pain. And on that day, the biggest championship for me was my faith and trust in God.

This was my first faith test. It *looked* like an athletic test, requiring me to jump over a bar and relying on gravity to help me have a successful jump. I had to jump headfirst, not worrying about what I could not see. When I landed, I knew I would land comfortably and safely on the mat.

Of course, that test taught me so much more.

Faith is very similar, asking us to trust God as we go forward each day on our mountain journey, not worrying about what we cannot see ahead. With faith, we must know that we are in the comforting care of God, and He will bring us safely over any mountain.

I needed this test. I am so thankful that I received it, and more importantly, I passed the test.

Had I not been able to connect my mountains back to this point, I would not have been able to share this book with you. Therefore, my biggest faith test and my first faith test were not about me but for those reading this book who need to be inspired, encouraged, and motivated. Most of all, these faith tests were for GOD'S GLORY!

The many trophies and awards I received in my ninth-grade year were lost in a last-minute family move. I wish I could touch once again the trophy for winning the athlete of the year award that I faithfully prayed to win. But even with the trophies and awards gone, I still have the relationship I began with God, and the experience of witnessing God's blessings and rewards through faith.

It was only because of my faith that I was able to overcome my fears, doubts, and frustrations from an injury that restricted me from competing to my best potential. This experience taught me what faith is all about and gave me a reference point for the rest of my life. I realize now that God was preparing me for the many life challenges that would await me, and because I knew what He was capable of doing, I never felt restricted again from being my best.

CHAPTER 4

STARTING WITH THE RIGHT ATTITUDE

I believe if you keep your faith, you keep your trust, you keep the right attitude, if you're grateful, you'll see God open up new doors.

– Joel Osteen

J ames 1:2 says, *Consider it pure joy, my brothers and sisters, whenever you face trials of many kinds* (NIV). The first time I read this verse, I glazed over what it meant and instantly allowed my mind to wonder: "Who can possibly find joy when faced with trials?" I know many positive people, but I thought to myself, *There is no possible way anyone can think around the mountain of challenges set before them and see the reward on the other side.*

Our minds far too often focus on the problem and not on the One who is the ultimate problem solver, God. We allow our emotions to control our thoughts, our thoughts to guide our attitude, and our attitude to drive our actions. Realistically, allowing our emotions to control our attitude is natural, because most of us have been conditioned through experiences to respond this way. However, allowing our attitude to get in front of the power of God and what He can do will lead to a dead end.

This conditioning results in happiness when things are good, misery when things go bad, and frustration when nothing seems to be going right. Uncontrolled emotions are not good, and the outcome of this lack of control represents every reason why it is so important for us to stay focused on God at all times. One should not expect to find joy with a bad attitude, and we certainly won't get a positive result with one either.

Attitudes Have Effects

One Sunday morning before church, Christian was playing with one of his toys when I asked him, "Have you made your bed?" He quickly responded that his bed was made. His response was not a complete shock because Christian often made his bed better than anyone in the house and required very little help. However, his bed had not been made. I returned to Christian and in a stern voice said, "Put the toy down and make your bed." Based on his reaction, you would have thought the world had come to an end. Christian took three minutes to climb the stairs, and I took the same three minutes to watch him walk to his room and do as I had asked. After five minutes, I went into Christian's room to check on his progress, only to find that he had done very little to his bed. I gave him additional time and told him, "I will be back in a few minutes, and I expect to see your bed made." When I returned, I was completely shocked! Christian's bed was the worst-made bed in the whole house. When I questioned why he did such a poor job, his response was, "I did good." He was so convinced of his work that he asked if I needed help making my bed.

Christian's experience taught me a couple of crucial lessons, including that we cannot expect the best outcome if we start with the wrong attitude. Christian's poor attitude tainted his ability to give his best, which caused him to be punished, losing his toys in the end.

Start with the Right Attitude

My experience with Christian prompted me to look back at how my attitude impacted my life experiences. I noticed a pattern. I was most successful when I approached my journeys of trials with the right attitude: thanksgiving and expectation.

> *Don't worry about anything; instead, pray about everything. Tell God what you need and thank him for all he has done.*
> **– Philippians 4:6 (NLT)**

Thanking God at the beginning of the journey shows that we are grateful for the things He has already done for us. Giving thanks for past blessings opens our hearts up to the expectancy of what God will do on the current journey. Thanking God opens our minds up to God's grace and takes us away from the negative thoughts that can trip us up before we get started. Additionally, thanking God serves as a reminder that He is our partner in this journey and that we are never alone.

Not only did I have a thankful heart, but I also faced those journeys by allowing God to hold my hand so that He could lead the way. I believe this is best done when we take a step back from the problem and allow God and His will to take the lead. This is my prayer: "God, I trust you to handle this problem while delivering me through this situation. God, what am I to learn from this?" Try it when you are facing your own faith challenge.

Letting God lead allows us to move the human nature of "self" out of the way, thus developing our attitude for the journey before us. I know for many people this is not an easy task. However, when we have the right attitude and remove ourselves from the storm, we allow room for God to deliver the optimal solutions.

The Impact of a Negative Attitude

Negative attitudes come in many forms – doubt, fear, unforgiveness, inadequacy, and anger – which can hold us back. Starting a journey of trials, adversities, and hardships with these negative attitudes can leave us stuck and trapped in a place that goes nowhere. Sure, maybe we can get a temporary grip on our negative attitudes by crying out to God as David does in the 150 chapters of the book of Psalms. Just as David did, we can go through many emotions when dealing with these negative attitudes; however, David always came back to God with, "I trust you." We are fortunate to have Scripture like those in Psalms to show us how to shift an attitude, how the right attitude leads to the fulfillment of God's promises, and how a heart that trusts God will always lead to a joyful journey's end.

Consider the Scripture telling how Jesus walked across the water to the frightened disciples, who were in a boat in a severe storm.

Between three and six o'clock in the morning, Jesus came to the disciples, walking on the water. When they saw him walking on the water, they were terrified. "It's a ghost!" they said, and screamed with fear. Jesus spoke to them at once. "Courage!" he said. "It is I. Don't be afraid!" Then Peter spoke up. "Lord, if it is really you, order me to come out on the water to you." "Come!" answered Jesus. So Peter got out of the boat and started walking on the water to Jesus. But when he noticed the strong wind, he was afraid and started to sink down in the water. "Save me, Lord!" he cried. At once Jesus reached out and grabbed hold of him and said, "What little faith you have! Why did you doubt?"

– Matthew 14:25–31 (GNT)

For Peter to come out of the boat, he had to trust Jesus enough to take that step of faith. As Peter stepped out of the boat onto the water, his attitude was in the right place, which was to go toward Jesus. However, once he took his eye off Jesus, he began to sink into the water. Peter's fear of the strong wind shifted his attitude. The storm came to test his faith.

When we trust God at all times during our faith journey, when we keep our focus on Him, we can reach toward God, knowing that He will be there to grab us when we need Him.

Mountains, much like storms, come not only to test our faith, but they also come to test our attitude toward God.

Trust in the LORD *with all your heart; do not depend on your own understanding. Seek his will in all you do, and he will show you which path to take.*

– Proverbs 3:5-6 (NLT)

A trusting attitude toward God is critical because the way we approach Him with our problem will set the tone for the direction we will take.

Questions for Reflection:

When you are faced with a mountain experience, what is your first tone or attitude?

- Do you go into panic mode?
- Do you look at the troubles and try to fix them yourself?
- Do you take your troubles to others first, hoping they will tell you how to solve them?

If you answered yes to any of these questions, know you are not alone. Many of us, when dealing with mountain experiences, suffer from worrying and the need to fix them ourselves. Worrying does nothing but drain the positive attitude out of you. As it says in Philippians 4:6, we are to "worry about nothing," but pray about everything.

Starting the Journey with an Attitude to Find God

As we start to climb our mountain of trials, adversities, and hardships, we want to make sure we have the right attitude for the journey, including an attitude that praises God and gives Him thanks. We must also have an attitude that realizes God is with us.

Through my mountain experiences, I learned that I had to first find God before focusing on the problem. If I focused on the problem first, I would bring the wrong attitudes like anxiety, fear, and doubt – no wonder, when the problem is all you can see. Even the thought of what we are dealing with can be too much weight for some of us to carry. By focusing on the challenges in front of our eyes and the emotions we are feeling, we tend to forget that God is there with us. Often, even seasoned believers tend to struggle with this because their focus is not on God, who is a spirit, but on the problem in front of them.

Here's a good illustration of how the right focus can impact our experience. Let's just imagine you are sitting in the airport waiting to board your plane for a business trip, but your flight is delayed because of stormy weather. Eventually, you board, and as your flight prepares to take off on the airport runway, the other passengers onboard are worried. You, however, remain calm because you know that once the plane flies above the storm and clouds, you will see nothing but the sun shining.

I will lift up mine eyes unto the hills, from whence cometh my help. My help cometh from the LORD, which made heaven and earth.

– Psalm 121:1-2 (KJV)

When we encounter storms in life, we may choose an attitude of calm and rise above the problem, which allows us to realize God is really there. When we do this, we get our bearings in the correct place and please God by finding and trusting Him first.

Renewing Our Mind for the Right Attitude

I am sure if I asked whether you know anyone who has a negative attitude towards most situations, you would more than likely say, "Yes."

Let's build on that question: "Why does that person have a negative attitude?" Your answer to this question might be you do not know, or you do not care.

Most negative attitudes are a result of life experiences. These unresolved experiences hurt our thought process, causing us to make decisions that don't provide a good result. Fortunately, when we are willing to work to make ourselves better, negative attitudes can be changed, and we can start our faith journey the correct way.

To successfully start our journey with the right attitude, we need to make sure we have all the ingredients that make up a healthy spiritual plan, which allows God to transform us for positive change. These ingredients are not hard to find and consist of prayer, fasting, reading Scripture, and meditation. As these ingredients are put together, the process of renewing our minds begin to take place. Spiritual plans that consist of these critical ingredients allow for good relationship-building with God, and consistently doing these things allows us an opportunity to communicate with and hear from God.

This is a good start, but to maximize the plan, we must allow God to transform us by the "renewing of our mind" as found in Romans 12:2. We must also allow Him to transform us by the "creation of a clean heart," which is found in Psalm 51:10. When we add a clean heart to a renewed mind, it's like adding a missing ingredient to our spirit, which allows our spirit to grow.

As our spirit grows, other people will start to notice a deeper inward growth in the form of fruit. Galatians 5:22 says that God reveals and provides this spiritual fruit: *love, joy, peace, patience, kindness, goodness, faithfulness, humility, and self-control.* This freely provided fruit helps to nourish our attitude, and as this fruit grows, we become more like Jesus, allowing the spirit to take over our old ways.

It's been said, "Trouble that finds us does not have to be the thing that defines us." I would add that it's the attitude that we carry during a time of trouble that makes us. Our first response to our mountain experiences can play a role in the outcome. The way we respond or usually react comes from our mindset or feeling at that time. With so many uncontrollable things going on around us, our minds can gravitate towards negativity. Keep in mind that the thing that comes in can very well be the thing that comes out. Therefore, it's important that we nurture the right attitude to develop the fruit we want.

> It's the attitude that we carry during a time of trouble that makes us.

Have an Attitude That Speaks Life

As we start our faith journey, we want to make sure our attitude is in the right place. To do this, we must take control of what is working within us, so that we can speak life out to others and our trials when they come. A perfect stranger (think: angel) taught me the transformative power of a right attitude.

I was having one of those negative days and was not feeling my very best. One day (because I am a polite Southerner), I casually asked a gentleman I did not know how he was. He responded, "I am fantastic!"

His response was very uplifting, and it changed my day. At that moment I chose to change what comes out of me when spoken to, realizing even if I do not feel fantastic, the more I speak it, I will eventually start to feel it.

My responses to a casual "how are you?" used to be negative. Now that I'm changing them, I can see how my life is changing.

I used to say, "I am just making it," but looking back, I now realize I had already made it.

Sometimes I would say, "Same old, same old," but now I realize I am not the same old person I used to be.

Maybe I said it's "just another day, "but as I think about it, I see all those days were blessed days.

Like anything we do, the more practice we have, the better we will be prepared. It took me some time to make the necessary change so that my responses could be what they are today, which is fantastic and amazing.

When our attitude leads our faith, it smooths the journey. These verses serve as good reminders for having the right attitude:

- *What we are suffering now is nothing compared with our future glory* (Romans 8:18 – NIRV).
- *And we know that God causes everything to work together for the good of those who love God and are called according to His purpose for them* (Romans 8:28 – NIRV).
- *"I alone know the plans I have for you, plans to bring you prosperity and not disaster, plans to*

bring about the future you hope for" (Jeremiah 29:11 – GNT).

- *Three different times I begged the Lord to take it away. Each time he said, "My grace is all you need. My power works best in weakness." So now I am glad to boast about my weaknesses, so that the power of Christ can work through me. That's why I take pleasure in my weaknesses and in the insults, hardships, persecutions, and troubles that I suffer for Christ. For when I am weak, then I am strong* (2 Corinthians 12:8-10 – NLT).
- *You must have the same attitude that Christ Jesus had* (Philippians 2:5 – NLT).
- *Even though you have not seen him, you love him. Though you do not see him now, you believe in him. You are filled with a glorious joy that can't be put into words* (1 Peter 1:8 – NIRV).
- *Your hearts and minds must be made completely new* (Ephesians 4:23 – GNT).

Now we can answer the question posed at the very beginning of this chapter. How can we find joy when we face our trials? You guessed it: with the right attitude!

Always be joyful because you belong to the Lord. I will say it again. Be joyful! Let everyone know how gentle you are. The Lord is coming soon. Don't worry about anything. No matter what happens, tell God about everything. Ask and pray, and give thanks to him. Then God's peace will watch over your hearts and your minds. He will do this because you belong to Christ Jesus. God's peace can never be completely understood. Finally, my brothers and sisters, always think about what is true. Think about what is noble,

right, and pure. Think about what is lovely and wor-
thy of respect. If anything is excellent or worthy of
praise, think about those kinds of things.

– Philippians 4:4-8 (NIRV)

My brothers and sisters, we can have joy when we face our trials by having forward-looking faith, when we focus on what our faith can produce ahead of our trials or mountain experiences. Forward-looking faith enables us to look ahead of our problem or situation, knowing that God has our back, and He does not want us to fail. Instead, He wants us to pass the test that is before us. We know God will always be there for us because His Word promises this over and over, as we find in Hebrews 13:5, *I will never leave you nor forsake you* (ESV). This promise should bring us joy when we are faced with trials.

When my children were younger and I promised to take them on vacation to Universal Studios or promised to reward them for getting good grades, they would become overjoyed with expectation and anticipation. They knew I would keep my promise. As our Father, God keeps His promise to us, His children. I am overjoyed when I think about what God will and can do during my test when I exercise my forward-looking faith.

Forward-looking faith encourages us to focus on the future reward for passing our faith test. It opens our imagination up to God's unlimited power and His will, which allows us to leave our trials behind. A negative attitude may creep up in the middle of a trial. However, we can trust that as long as we continue to grow in our faith, by the time negativity arrives, it won't be able to survive because we have trained the mind with a positive attitude.

Remember this: keeping a right attitude at the beginning of your mountain experience lets God know that you trust Him and that your faith is expecting Him to move on your behalf according to His will.

> Keeping a right attitude at the beginning of your mountain experience lets God know that you trust Him.

Attitude Check Exercise

When you find yourself going into a negative mindset, write down three positive things God has done for you in the past. Think family, career, friends, and daily events. It can be something as simple as:

- Yesterday traffic was lighter than normal. I got home from work fifteen minutes sooner, and I could spend more time with my wife and kids.
- I finished college without much debt, mainly because my mother told me that having a lot of debt could hurt my ability to get a loan for a car or house.
- When I was in college, God blessed me with a great mentor who would not let me quit school when my grades were bad.

Your attitude at the beginning of a faith test is key. It's where great things begin.

– Eddie Johnson

CHAPTER 5

WALKING WITH PATIENCE

Let nothing disturb you.
Let nothing frighten you.
All things pass away:
God never changes.
Patience obtains all things.
Those who have God
Find they lack nothing;
God alone suffices.
— St. Teresa of Avila

Trusting God during a mountain experience is a critical attitude that will set the tone for the direction we will take. That trust will help us build the patience that will carry us to the completion of our test and the reward that awaits us in the end.

Patience is defined as "the ability to continue doing something for a long time without losing interest, especially something difficult; the ability to wait for a long time without becoming angry or upset; and the ability to accept situations that you do not

> Trusting God during a mountain experience is a critical attitude that will set the tone for the direction we will take.

like." A person with patience is calm, has self-control, can wait for an extended period for something, and can go with the flow and not be easily bothered.

Patience is a tough attitude to develop. Different versions of the Bible describe patience as perseverance, endurance, and long-suffering. When we demonstrate patience, we are saying, "Regardless of what the mountain looks like, I am going to wait on God and His will, even if I must suffer for a while as I am going through this mountain experience."

Patience is one of the nine fruit of the spirit, the attributes that all Christians should be working to develop in their life once the Holy Spirit enters in after being saved. Patience comes only through the Holy Spirit. We can't just wake up one morning and say we "got it." And we certainly can't buy it, as we do for just about everything else.

Developing patience may take a long time – years even! Many people need a great deal of endurance while on their faith test. This endurance teaches us to trust God more, allowing our faith to grow. We must draw closer to God and rely on Him; only with God's help will we have the strength for the journey.

Why Patience Is Important

Patience allows us to put our emotions and feelings aside, which allows God to take control. When we do this, we can make a clear decision directed by God. Emotions, when removed, make way for a direct shot to happiness, peace, and the blessings that God has for us. Then we can witness just how much He loves us.

We don't want to get ahead of God on our journey. Patience teaches us to allow Him to lead us. Taking the lead over our mountain experiences could be a set-up for a disaster, which might destroy us.

> *The Lord is good to everyone who trusts in him, So it is best for us to wait in patience—to wait for Him to save us—And it is best to learn this patience in our youth. When we suffer, we should sit along in silent patience.*
>
> **– Lamentations 3:25-28 (GNT)**

The sooner we learn to trust God and wait on Him, the better we understand that His ways are not our ways. When we learn to wait on the Lord, it slows us down. We do not make quick and sudden moves that can hurt our life.

A friend was having some challenges at work, and a new company offered him a job. Signs indicated that taking the new job might not be the best decision. The new company was unclear about their need for the position for which he had applied. When he went to complete his new-hire paperwork, the office administrator hinted that there was a lot of disorganization in the company. He also was given inconsistent start dates by different managers in the new company. I shared that I felt God was telling my friend not to go anywhere.

However, my friend lacked patience, and he was not willing to wait on God. Even with these concerning issues, my friend decided to take the new job so he could get away from the challenges at his current place of employment.

He encountered several mishaps. No manager was there to greet him on his first day of work, and his new coworkers did not know who he was. Because my friend did not slow down, he did not get the offer in writing, and the salary he was offered was not honored. The hiring manager was fired shortly after my friend's first day.

Had my friend learned patience, it is possible he could have stayed at his old job and even received the promotion for which he was being considered. As 2 Peter 3:9 says, *The Lord is not slow to do what He has promised as some think; instead He is patient with you because He does not want anyone to be destroyed ....* (GNT). In this same way, we want to be patient so we do not get ahead of ourselves and miss the blessing that God has for us. If only my friend had understood this at the time.

Patience allows us to mature spiritually and be complete in our Christian walk. We have to look at patience in the same way that a farmer looks at his crop. The farmer cannot sell his crop until it is ripe and ready, which, depending on the type of crop, may take some time to be ready for the market. It is the same way with us. God cannot and will not give us our blessing until it is ready and we are prepared to receive it. If it is given to us too soon, we may push it to the side, throw it away, or not realize it is there.

While waiting on God's timing to deliver, we must always be patient while we are traveling on our faith journey. Our waiting should be like a woman who is pregnant and expecting a child. A woman knows going into a pregnancy that the optimal time for delivery is nine months. If she delivers too soon, her blessing and the long-awaited child may have complications or come with health issues. Knowing this, she does not rush the nine months; however, during this time she does everything to prepare for her blessing. Yes, during this nine months she may experience discomfort, and it may come with difficulties, but she has patience and waits with great joy because she knows that her waiting will result in a blessing.

Knowing that God is preparing everything for us and working everything out for our good, we should be praising God as we continue on our mountain experience and wait with patience.

Causes of Impatience

Patience is not easy; most of us struggle with it every day. Mountain experiences can be such a challenge, making patience hard, because when a storm comes along, the darkness can often bring fear. When fear is present, we desire to hurry past it as quickly as possible. The only way we can deal with fear in a dark moment is by finding some light.

No, I am not speaking of the light that comes from a candle, a flashlight, or a light bulb. I am speaking of the best light made available to us, which can be found in God.

"Lord, you are my lamp. You bring light into my darkness."
– 2 Samuel 22:29 (NIRV)

The Lord is my light and my salvation; whom shall I fear? The Lord is the strength of my life; of whom shall I be afraid?
– Psalm 27:1 (KJV)

I love a song by William Murphy called "Everlasting God:" "…the Lord's my light and salvation. Whom shall I fear? Of whom shall I be afraid? I will wait on you. I will trust in you."

So to find the light we need, to lose our fear, we must trust that God is with us, wait on Him to reveal His light in His time. There is no darkness that God's light cannot penetrate.

Waiting for patience can be challenging. That's why it's called "impatience!" However, when we wait out our mountain experience with God operating as our instructor and guide, we are better positioned for something good from Him. If we hurry, it can harm us.

If we believe we can trust ourselves to deal with our mountain experience better and take matters into our own hands, we can make mistakes. This individual control can cause us to get ahead of God and lead to the contamination of our blessings.

Fear, anxiousness, and a "right now" mindset can drive us to try to take control and manipulate our mountain experience. This mindset causes us to get ahead of God. God operates according to His plan and perfect will, and if we try to manipulate that plan, we put God in a position to allow us to do what we want. But remember: God's plan is always better than ours, making our personal plan invalid in His eyes. Our manipulation can cause the journey to shift from God's plan, stalling our blessings or causing us to miss them.

If you feel a need for control, stop for a moment and refocus your mind and attitude back on God. If this is a struggle, pull out the list you wrote of positive things God has done for you. (See the chapter on attitude for a reminder.) This will remind you that you are successful only if God is a part of your journey. You can then begin to release the need for control and allow God to lead you through your mountain experience.

These verses can help you restore a right attitude and grow patience:

- Fear: *For I, the LORD your God, hold your right hand; it is I who say to you, "Fear not, I am the one who helps you"* (Isaiah 41:13 – ESV).
- Anxiousness: *Do not be anxious about anything, but in everything by prayer and supplication with thanksgiving let your requests be made known to God* (Philippians 4:6 – ESV).
- A right-now mindset: *Don't copy the behavior and customs of this world, but let God transform you into a new person by changing the way you think. Then you will learn to know God's will for you, which is good and pleasing and perfect* (Romans 12:2 – NLT).

Questions for Reflection:

If you think you may be rushing your mountain experience, ask these questions:

What am I missing by moving too fast?
Will I miss God's best by going at this pace?
Does my soul feel at spiritual peace?
Is God leading the way, or am I asking God to catch up with me?

Growing Patience through Long-Suffering

People say they want patience, but few are willing to do what is necessary to grow it. In other words, they won't ask God for help. Many fear that praying for patience could require that they suffer through a situation. Sometimes we must suffer for some time – think "long-suffering" – while God works for our good. However, please know that while we are suffering through a mountain experience, God will sustain and keep us. He will guide us through any landmines we might encounter along our journey up the mountain. God will provide us with the wisdom we need to withstand all things we will face.

If we think we can gain patience without enduring long-suffering, we are saying we want the reward that comes from having patience but do not want to put in the work that produces it.

Since we do not know how long our period of long-suffering will last, the best thing we can do is praise and worship our way through it. Continual praise will bring peace during the storm.

Things to Consider for Growing Patience

- **Have the right attitude for the journey.** When your attitude is in the right place, you will find joy in God. *My brothers and sisters, you will face all kinds of trouble. When you do, think of it as pure joy. Your faith will be tested. You know that when this happens, it will produce in you the strength (patience) to continue* (James 1:2-3 – NIRV).
- **Submit your mountain experience to God.** Knowing that God cares, we must be willing

to trust our trials, adversities, and hardships to Him and trust His plan for us through the journey. 1 Peter 5:7 says, *Leave all your worries with him, because he cares for you* (GNT). Proverbs 3:5-6 says, *Trust in the Lord with all thine heart, and lean not unto thine own understanding. In all thy ways acknowledge him, and he shall direct thy paths* (KJV).

- **Be willing to finish the test so that God will get the glory.** No matter how long it takes, we must be open to staying the course until the journey is over, knowing that God will work everything out for our good and for His glory. Acts 20:24 says, *But my life means nothing to me. My only goal is to finish the race. I want to complete the work the Lord Jesus has given me. He wants me to tell others about the good news of God's grace* (NIRV). Romans 8:28 says, *And we know that all things work together for good to them that love God, to them who are the called according to his purpose* (KJV).

Questions for Reflection:

The next time you are struggling with patience, I want you to answer these questions:

> Has God been impatient with me?
> Has God ever punished me before I sinned or committed a wrong?

If you answered *no* to these questions, then the next time you want to get ahead of God, you should think about saying no. Saying no allows you to be patient with your mountain and not overreact to what you are dealing with.

In conclusion, patience put into action shows just how much we trust God, His timing, and His will for our faith journey. The best example of patience I can share with you is God's patience with us to acknowledge that His son, Jesus, died for our sins so that we could have everlasting life.

> **Patience put into action shows just how much we trust God.**

Patience through our faith test allows us to witness just how much God loves us.

– Eddie Johnson

CHAPTER 6

HEARING GOD'S VOICE

God speaks to those who take time to listen, and He listens to those who take time to pray.

– Our Daily Bread

Several years ago, when my daughter Kennedy was about eight years old, she came running to me full of excitement. "Dad! Dad!" she exclaimed, "I need to tell you something. But before you say anything, I need you to listen until I am done." After she finished and walked away, I went into my room and broke down in tears. My only daughter, whom I love very much, just told me I don't listen, and this cut me like a Ninja with multiple swords.

Kennedy is the last person I want to feel this way. In fact, I want her to talk with me about *anything*. But if she does not think I would listen, why would she come to me? And what about Christian and Cameron? As a father, I felt like I was failing. What about my family, friends, employees, and coworkers? At that moment I realized I must do something to fix this, and fix it quick.

Several months later, I started a journey through my job that focused on servant leadership. We read *The Servant* by James C. Hunter, which teaches that the foundation of leadership is built on relationships, love, service, and sacrifice.

For a year, we were charged with working on our two weakest leadership attributes, and this was my opportunity to work on becoming a better listener. A year later, I had the opportunity to lead and mentor about sixty associates who also wanted to become better listeners.

What a blessing this book and journey was! As I was working to become a better listener and mentoring others to do so, I learned how to hear God's voice better.

I realized that we cannot hear God's voice unless we are listening for it. To listen, we must first

> **We cannot hear God's voice unless we are listening for it.**

make a choice to do so, and then we must focus and concentrate on what He says to understand what we are hearing.

As we are taking the journey through our mountain experiences of trials, many of us are searching for answers for our faith test, and we want so desperately to hear God's voice. However, we are moving so much that we fail to hear Him when He speaks, or we misunderstand what He says.

Many of us wait every day hoping to hear a knock at the door and find God standing there with a quick answer to how we should deal with our challenges. We expect Him to arrive in the midst of a troubling circumstance, and just like a coach or a parent, tell us in an audible voice what to do. The problem with focusing on hearing an audible voice is that we fail to hear God's voice.

God speaks to us through the Holy Spirit, which we receive once we accept Christ as the Lord and Savior of our life. Since God speaks through the Holy Spirit, we receive the understanding that He wants us to have, not the understanding that comes from somewhere else.

So to help us overcome this human error of listening for an audible voice from God, we must slow down enough to focus and concentrate on what God is saying. Only then can we understand what we are hearing. When I say slow down, I mean, stop, be still, and remain silent.

Not only have I learned some good things about listening from Kennedy, but I have also learned from my son Cameron as well. All my kids are pretty good athletes, and they are very competitive. One day, Cameron and I were talking about his upcoming basketball season. I said how proud I was that his grades had improved from the last quarter. I told Cameron that he should remember this moment because the most important thing was school and not sports. His response? "Dad, you said God was the most important thing!"

To my surprise, Cameron had been listening to everything I had been telling him, his brother, and sister, and I did not know it. Cameron heard my voice and was paying attention to the things I had said, and he understood what he had heard me say, which was that God was the most important thing.

Just like Cameron, we should be listening with the intent to understand what we hear from God.

"Pay close attention to what you hear. The closer you listen, the more understanding you will be given—and you will receive even more."

– Mark 4:24 (NLT)

God's Silence

Silence used to be challenging for me. The toughest and most frustrating thing about silence was when it came from others. Getting the silent treatment from a friend or from someone I wanted an answer from would burn me up. I am not alone in this feeling, because most of us hate getting the silent treatment.

If you don't think you have an issue with getting the silent treatment, let me ask you this question. *What if silence and the feeling of being ignored came from God? Would that change your feelings about silence?*

We have all experienced a time when we thought God was silent to us, especially when we needed something or we were dealing with our mountain experiences. When we need something right away, we want an answer immediately. We think we don't have time to wait for a reply.

It took me some time to understand why God would appear to be silent; after all, He knew I needed an answer from Him. I have come to realize that God's silence can be a good thing. God's silence during our mountain experience trains us to seek Him more.

When it seems that God is silent, we should look at it like this: when we were in school and the teacher had taught for several weeks, the teacher gave us a test at the end of the lesson to see what we had learned. As we were taking the test, the teacher was silent; however, the teacher was watching us during the testing period.

From a spiritual perspective, sometimes God will be silent while we are going through our faith test. As God is watching, He is allowing us the opportunity to show Him that we have learned to trust Him on this faith journey. Once we have passed this part of our test, we are elevated on our journey to the next level and prepared for the next test that lies ahead as we continue to climb our mountain.

We must never forget that every test we face, God has equipped and prepared us to pass.

> *No test or temptation that comes your way is beyond the course of what others have had to face. All you need to remember is that God will never let you down; he'll never let you be pushed past your limit; he'll always be there to help you come through it.*
>
> **– 1 Corinthians 10:13 (MSG)**

When we are in a hurry, God's silence can seem as though it is the worst, causing us to be very frustrated. Believe me, God is aware of all things, and His choice to be silent could be an effort to grab our attention. It could be that the frustration of God's silence is designed to get us to slow down our journey so that we will stop talking, be still, and silently wait to listen for His voice.

How to Know God's Voice

Just like the silence we often get from God, we have to be silent with ourselves so that we can hear.

We know that prayer is a simple act of communicating with God, and I am sure many of you pray very well. However, do you ever stop communicating with God so that He can communicate with you? God can talk all day, and His voice will appear muted if we don't just stop, be still, and silently listen for what He has to say. No one can hear multiple conversations or sounds and say they understand everything they heard. So what do you want to hear? Is it clutter over God or God over clutter? The voice of man over God or God over the voice of man?

We must choose because we cannot do both. As Psalm 46:10 states, *Be still, and know that I am God* (KJV).

The key to listening for God's voice can be found in our silence, which requires us to be still and have quality quiet time with Him. God desires an intimate relationship with us just as much as we want it with Him. When we pull away

> **The key to listening for God's voice can be found in our silence.**

from all the distractions of this world and focus our attention on Him, we will find that God has something to say. Remember that God will speak at the right time; therefore, you may not get an answer right away.

Quiet time is the time we find to spend alone in silence with God. During this time of silence with God, we should be listening and reading His Word. Listening and reading Scripture is so important because God will not move our spirit to do anything that is against what His Word says. If unsure what to read or where to find an answer, just ask God to direct you to what He wants you to read and hear.

John 10:27 states, *"My sheep hear my voice, and I know them, and they follow me* (KJV). Quiet time allows us to build on the relationship we have with God, thus allowing us to know His voice the best. The relationship we continue to build helps keep us in tune with Him so that His voice can be heard over the clutter of those things that distract us from His blessings.

As I think back to when I was a kid with my friends, I can remember times when I was about to do something wrong. I would hear this little voice that sounded like my mother saying, "I did not raise you to make decisions like that." No, my mother was nowhere around. However, I have a very deep relationship with her and we can talk about anything. It was as if she was there watching what I was doing. In the same way, our relationship with God is critical to our listening because it heightens our ability to hear Him better.

God speaks to us through the Holy Spirit, but I don't want you to think that God only uses words to talk. When God speaks, He knows exactly how to get our attention, and He has different ways to send us His message. He may speak to some while they are still and silent, He may use a conversation with a friend or even a stranger, or He may use a situation. My mother tends to hear God best when water is running, and I tend to hear God speaking through the words from gospel songs. In whatever way God chooses to speak to you, just know He wants you to hear Him.

Not knowing when God is speaking to you can have consequences, but knowing His voice can be rewarding. Let me share a story from my own life.

When Treza and I moved in 1999 to Atlanta, I hoped to find employment with some big company in downtown Atlanta that would include stock options in an incentive package. About three months into my job search, I received a call from CJ, a former coworker, who told me the company where we had worked together was looking for a manager in Atlanta. He said my name kept coming up. I told CJ not to give my number to anyone because I had no desire to return to the company.

Another month went by, and I finally received a job offer with a company in downtown Atlanta. I was interested, but it wasn't that plum job with the juicy incentives I wanted. I decided to speak with the hiring manager at my former company to find out what they were looking for and express some concerns from my first two years of employment. To my surprise, I never needed to address my concerns. I learned from the initial conversation that they were willing to do some things differently for me than before, and this helped ease my concerns.

Following that meeting, I prayed and asked God to show me what He wanted for me. The next day I began to see the answer to my prayers. Every day for a week, God allowed me to see trucks belonging to my previous employer. This was interesting because for the four months I had been in Atlanta, I had not seen this company's name anywhere.

Then the other company that had offered me a job called to rescind the offer.

I took all of this as God's way of telling me that His will was for me to go back and work for my former company. Around the time I returned to the company, I found out we were expecting our first child, Kendall. Going back to work for my former company was important because God knew what mountain would be standing in front of me in the years ahead.

The company was a major blessing to my family and me, providing the love and support I would need after Kendall was diagnosed with a brain tumor. To have the flexibility to go to appointments when necessary and close my office door to pray or just cry out to God was invaluable to me personally. To receive a handwritten letter from my CEO and calls periodically from several other executives in the company meant so much to my family and me. God knew what I needed according to His plan for my life, and still to this day, I am extremely grateful to the company for what they did for me. There is no telling what I would have dealt with if I worked for another company during that time. More than anything, I am so happy that my relationship with God was close enough that I could hear His voice when I saw the company trucks and accept His guidance over my desires and what I thought would be best.

Question for Reflection:

What are the ways that God speaks to you so that you can hear His voice?

Challenges and Difficulties with Hearing God's Voice

It is amazing how we can hear the littlest of things around us: nature, words hidden in a song, or whispered gossip. However, when God is speaking....

No, let me put it this way. When we know God is speaking to get our attention, we act as though we did not hear Him. Why of all things would we miss God's voice? Is it because when God speaks, His language is something we don't understand? How about because when God speaks, His words sound crazy to us. Could it be because we don't recognize His voice? Is it possible that we don't want to hear God so that we can do things our way? Can it be that we are the problem —not God? We all have missed God's voice, and many of us still do on a regular basis.

Not long ago, a friend who was struggling with some family issues needed my advice. He believed God had spoken to him about forgiveness, and he knew it was important that he forgive some family members. However, he felt there was no need to waste time forgiving a wrong that had been, sadly, committed over and over. My friend planned to wait several months to see if it would happen again. He went on to tell me he knew what God was telling him to do, but since he felt at peace with his decision, he did not feel it was necessary to forgive.

After hearing the situation in detail, I did not feel comfortable giving my opinion or a response until I got an answer to a question that was troubling me. I asked my friend this simple question: "Do you know how God speaks to you?" The response concerned me.

"Yes, God gives me peace with what I am doing."

Many of us share this same mentality as my friend, and sadly, we miss the most important point of hearing God's voice: to allow Him to tell us what we should be doing. Since my friend felt putting his agenda ahead of God and doing things his way was the correct way, I had to ask some follow-up questions.

"Is God giving you peace, or are you giving yourself temporary peace? Who told you that you needed to forgive?"

It was evident to me that my friend did not want to forgive, even though God had told him to. I told my friend that God will not give peace to a pre-approved agenda that He had nothing to do with and was against what He told him to do. It was obvious to me that my friend's struggling family issues were the result of the unforgiveness he held in his heart. At that point, I thought to myself: how could he have missed this?

So, let's go back to my question: Why, of all things, would we miss God's voice?

The reason is simple; it's disobedience. Disobedience comes from our failure to trust and obey God's will, putting our agenda above Him. When we are disobedient too long, God's voice seems to get lower and lower until it appears mute. No, God is not speaking differently than He was before. However, our ears start to hear more of the world and less of Him.

The blessing is that we don't have to live in this muted state of hearing. The way to deal with disobedience is first to ask God to reveal to you what you are disobedient about. Next, we need to repent and acknowledge to God the concern that is driving our disobedience. This could be anything from fear, not feeling worthy, or feeling ill-equipped to do what He wants us to do.

God hears us, and because of His unconditional love, He will restore and give us what we need to overcome anything. If God did not think we were capable of doing what He has given us to do, He would not have given it to us.

I've been on both sides of this. I've been on the side of "I hear you, Lord, and I'm going do what you told me to do even though I don't understand it." Also, I've even been on the other side of "I hear you, Lord but…"

What if Moses allowed his "but…I don't feel equipped to go before Pharaoh and bring the Israelites out of Egypt" to cause him to be disobedient to God? How about if the Israelites allowed their "but…we don't think Moses is worthy enough to take us into the promised land" to hinder them?

> *Be careful that you do not refuse to listen to the One who is speaking. For if the people of Israel did not escape when they refused to listen to Moses, the earthly messenger, we will certainly not escape if we reject the One who speaks to us from heaven!*
>
> **– Hebrews 12:25 (NLT)**

The three-letter word "but" is long enough to be a distraction that can trip us up into disobedience every time. Therefore, we need to be careful of our "but…" when God is speaking.

Disobedience of any kind can cause us to miss what we need to hear from God. When we miss His voice, it delays the promises and rewards He has stored up for us.

Questions for Reflection:

What promise(s) has God made to you that are being delayed by your disobedience?

Because of disobedience, what rewards have you delayed because you missed God's voice?

Earlier we talked about quiet time, and if you don't practice this on a regular basis, you will find it hard to do. Our world has us always on the go and involved in so many things that finding quiet time is difficult. However, just like anything else we desire to do, if we put in a little bit of training, added with determination, quiet time can become the new normal for our day.

Developing Quiet Time Exercise

- Day 1 – Day 2

  After your prayer time, sit in silence for two minutes. Try not to concentrate on anything, especially things that may be concerning you, and spend time reading scripture after your silence.

- Day 3 – Day 4

  After your prayer time, sit in silence for three minutes. Try not to concentrate on anything, especially things that may be concerning you, and spend time reading scripture after your silence.

- Day 5 – Day 6

  After your prayer time, sit in silence for four minutes. Try not to concentrate on anything, especially things that may be concerning you, and spend time reading scripture after your silence.

- Day 7

  After your prayer time, sit in silence for five minutes. Try not to concentrate on anything, especially things that may be concerning you, and spend time reading scripture after your silence.

For the remaining days to follow, continue to build on your quiet time, allowing your relationship with God to grow stronger. Quiet time with God may require a sacrifice of your time. If you have a family, this may be a challenge. So if it means getting up five to ten minutes earlier in the morning before anything troubles your mind and heart, make the sacrifice. This small sacrifice will open your ears more to God's voice and His love for you.

The key to hearing God can be found in our stillness and silence.

– Eddie Johnson

CHAPTER 7
RECEIVING THE REWARD

A season of suffering is a small assignment when compared to the reward. Rather than begrudge your problem, explore it. Ponder it. And most of all, use it. Use it to the glory of God.

– Max Lucado

One of my mottos and standards to live by is, "We are blessed to be a blessing to others." It pulls my heartstrings when I witness others giving a gift to someone in need and see the excitement it brings.

"I will make you into a great nation. And I will bless you. I will make your name great. You will be a blessing to others."

– Genesis 12:1 (NIRV)

I also enjoy it when I witness someone recognized with a reward for service to others or an achievement they have accomplished. In both situations, someone is giving or receiving a blessing, and it is the blessings that pull at my heart.

Which of these blessings do you like to receive?

A. Gifts

B. Rewards

C. Both A and B

D. None of the above

If I had to guess, your answer was not D. We all like to receive the blessings that come with gifts and rewards, and they frequently come as a surprise. Blessings make us feel good, especially when they come after a disappointing situation, feelings of hurt and pain, or a hard time. Blessings are especially sweet when they originate from a family member, friend, or someone who was just thinking about you. Blessings make us feel good, they encourage us, and they make us feel loved.

So let me ask you: What if your blessing came from God? How would you feel then?

I can tell you that every time God blesses me, I feel overwhelming joy because, once again, God has blessed me above my expectations and imagination. As it says in Ephesians 3:20: *To him who by means of his power working in us is able to do so much more than we can ever ask for, or even think of* (GNT).

God has blessed me in many ways for my faithfulness and trust. Every blessing was always greater than the feelings or emotions that I may have been experiencing while I was going over and through my mountain experiences.

The reward comes when we have moved up and over the mountain. And while the rewards are nice and appreciated, knowing that we passed the test because of our faith is just as rewarding.

Because you know all this, you have great joy. You have joy even though you may have had to suffer for a little while. You may have had to suffer sadness in all kinds of trouble. Your troubles have come in order to prove that your faith is real. Your faith is worth more than gold. That's because gold can pass away even when fire has made it pure. Your faith is meant to bring praise, honor, and glory to God. This will happen when Jesus Christ returns.

– 1 Peter 1:6-7 (NIRV)

When we have passed the test of faith, the reward of knowing we have grown in our relationship with God and proven our faith to be real should bring us great joy. Through our praise, we show deep gratitude toward God for His faithfulness to us while we were on the journey.

> **Through our praise, we show deep gratitude toward God for His faithfulnes.**

Blessed is the person who keeps on going when times are hard. After they have come through hard times, this person will receive a crown. The crown is life itself. The Lord has promised it to those who love him.

– James 1:12 (NIRV)

The ultimate reward promised is the crown of life to those who love the Lord. Knowing that God has never broken a promise should keep us focused until we receive our reward here on earth and in our eternal life. To be rewarded for our faith is a blessing, and blessings come from God's grace.

Question for Reflection:

What have you trusted God for that resulted in a reward filled with blessings?

Rewards as the Result of Our Faith

One of the most disturbing feelings in life is when you learn that someone has used you for their gain. They may have used you for money, personal belongings, advancement of their career, or to promote their agenda. Often when I was used, I wanted to retaliate, even though no real harm was done. Instead, as a believer, I took my concern to God and let Him work it out for me.

Let's look differently at being used. When we come up against our mountains, we know that God can move them on our behalf every time, making life a smooth journey full of rewards. However, let's be honest; we all know this will not always be the case.

Could it be that God does not move our mountains so He can use us for His Kingdom? Could it be that God is not moving our mountains so we can grow in our faith or simply activate our faith?

The Bible tells us of the rewards of faith. For example, the woman with the issue of blood had faith she would be healed if she could just touch the clothes of Jesus. Even after losing everything he had, Job kept his faith in God, and he was rewarded with twice as much as he had lost. Daniel was not harmed in the lion's den. Shadrach, Meshach, and Abednego were delivered from the fiery furnace.

So how might God reward our faith? The rewards we receive after passing a faith test are blessings many of us do not often think about. These blessings can, of course, be just for us; however, the blessings can be for others as well.

When we see a family member, neighbor, friend, or coworker pass a faith test, it has the power to inspire us to desire a better walk and relationship with God than we currently may have.

As others witness our journey, many may be glad they did not get our challenging mountain as their assignment. It may even be downright fearful to watch, even from a distance. While they are watching, they may be wondering how we will get through this mountain.

Traveling these mountains can be bad for our health, causing our bodies to look worn down and beaten up. However, because of God's grace, when others look at us, they can see a Christ-like image in us, the reward of our faith.

There was a time I used to wonder "why me" when I experienced my mountains. Now, thanks to my growth and the blessings of God, my attitude is "why not me?" God has always blessed me above my expectations, wishes, and desires after I passed a faith test. Knowing what God has done for me before allows me to remain focused on what He can do again and again, as long as I continue trusting Him no matter what.

Realizing the Reward After the Test

No one can please God without faith, for whoever comes to God must have faith that God exists and rewards those who seek him.

– Hebrews 11:6 (GNT)

I have learned that we cannot fully appreciate the blessing without first recognizing that we passed the test of faith. I have also learned that through our faith and seeking God, our mountain experiences can be blessings waiting to be revealed.

> Our mountain experiences can be blessings waiting to be revealed.

When Kendall was diagnosed with the brain tumor, I only knew to seek God for strength and rely on my faith. Even with the roller-coaster emotions, the doubts and fears that tried to consume me, I never gave up my faith in God for Kendall to be healed. Even as his body was slowly declining, in my heart, I knew he got the healing he needed.

After Kendall passed away, I knew I had entertained an angel. Kendall had completed his assignment, and God needed him for something else. I am glad I never gave up my trust in what God could do. *My faith reward from God was the birth of Kennedy and being blessed sixteen months later with Christian and Cameron.* Being blessed like this let me know just how much God loved me.

As I look back to my first faith test in the ninth grade, I realize that my injury was the best thing to ever happen to me. Of course, I missed the opportunity for a basketball career. But my injury taught me to have faith and to experience the rewards: winning the championship in the high jump and then ultimately winning athlete of the year. After my hand injury, I could not play the trombone, so I switched to the bass drum. My peers voted me the most outstanding bandsman of the year.

These experiences from ninth grade laid the foundation of my faith and strength, and they prepared me for the biggest test of my faith with Kendall.

Questions for Reflection:

What mountain have you faced that you feared would take your dream away, cause you to lose everything, or stress you out? How did it turn into a blessing waiting to be revealed?

Our faith tests leave us treasures that last forever. We grow our relationship with God; we learn to trust Him with blinded eyes and rely on His strength; we learn beyond doubt that He will protect us as promised on our journey. These treasures remind us of God's love, grace, and mercy. And we want to carry these lessons of faith with us as we approach new mountains that lie ahead.

You will not fully appreciate the blessings, which comes from God's grace, without first recognizing that you passed the test of faith.

– Eddie Johnson

CHAPTER 8

CONCLUSION

Our mountain experiences are designed to bring us a more intimate relationship with God, allowing us to trust Him more and strengthening our faith.

These mountains are designed for our good and bring rewards or blessings from God here and in Heaven. Also, we must remember to give God the glory, honor, and praise during and after the completion of our faith test.

Our mountains can be painful at times, making us ask, "Why is this happening to me?" They can even appear to last for way too long, leaving us to wonder when God will come to our rescue. *Will* He come?

These are legitimate questions, and everyone has them. But remember: God promised never to leave us or forsake us.

As you read through this book, you may have noticed that the key to passing the test of faith starts with our relationship with God. As our relationship grows, our trust in God grows. As our trust grows, we strengthen our commit-

> **The key to passing the test of faith starts with our relationship with God.**

ment to the right attitude, knowing that God will not let us down no matter what. Growing trust increases our patience as we wait on God's timing and purpose for our life. Trust in God opens us up to listening and obeying Him, even when it may not make sense.

We can activate our faith each time we are faced with a mountain experience, and when our faith is put into action, He promises to deliver us a reward that no one can take away. As you can see, having a relationship with God is critical for our faith journey.

I get great joy as a father, remembering that saying The Lord's Prayer with Kendall every day opened the door for his relationship with God. I truly believe that as my family and friends gathered with us regularly to pray for Kendall, he was praying for us.

My ninth-grade basketball injury was not designed to take my dreams away, as I once thought. Yes, I won many awards that year and even won the champion-ship in the high jump when the odds were against me. The injury was designed so that I could first develop a relationship with God and be a champion for Him. The disappointment, hurt, and pain from my injury and then winning the championship enabled me to be a champion and have a love for others going through similar feelings.

... (v.2) I may have all the faith needed to move mountains—but if I have no love, I am nothing.

(v.13) Meanwhile, these three remain: faith, hope, and love; and the greatest of these is love.
– 1 Corinthians 13:2,13 (GNT)

My mother taught me the power of faith in action when I was a teenager. She taught me how to love God and other people. She taught me the meaning of faith and what faith does when I put it into action. I am filled with a sense of gratitude and humility. My mother's lessons were by far the biggest blessing of my life.

PRAYER OF GRATITUDE

Father God, I come before you with a humble heart to once again say thank you. Thank you for your mercy, your grace, and believing in me when at times I did not believe in myself.

I also ask that you forgive me, Lord, for being slow to accept and finish the assignment of writing this book.

Lord, on May 12, 2017, I heard you loud and clear when I read your Word in Acts 20:24, *But my life means nothing to me. My only goal is to finish the race. I want to complete the work the Lord Jesus has given me. He wants me to tell others about the good news of God's grace* (NIRV).

Thank you, Lord, for trusting me with this assignment. You know how many times I wanted to give up. You could have reassigned this to someone else, but you stayed with me and continued to increase the burning in my heart.

Lord, the time we have spent together, with you as the author and me as the pen for this book, has meant more to me than anything in my life. Lord, I have cried many tears because I know I could not have put this many words together without your inspiration.

Lord, you have opened my eyes to see new things and my heart to explore different feelings and emotions. I will never forget this time as long as I live.

In all the times I had no one to turn to, you were waiting for me to come into your arms so you could show your love for me. Thank you, Lord, for all the good and tough times, because it's in those tough times that I have come to know you better, trust you more, and love you with all my heart.

Lord, I hope and pray that I did not miss any words in this book and that it is pleasing in your sight. God, I pray that even a simple glimpse of this book will move hearts, open minds, and save souls. Lord, I want others to witness the promises and rewards you have for them as a result of their faith in you. More than anything, God, I pray that others will be overjoyed with your love, realize your presence, and trust you more than ever before.

Lord, I know it's not my job to change anyone, but I know some are called to plant the seed and some are to water. Whatever my role is, let it be. Use me as you choose. I just want to make a difference for your kingdom and fulfill my purpose for your glory.

Thank you for the blessings of Kendall, Kennedy, Christian, and Cameron and trusting them into my care.

I thank you, Lord, in Jesus' name. Amen!

ABOUT THE AUTHOR

Eddie L. Johnson is an author, speaker, life coach, and servant leader, who brings joy and life to difficult situations. An encourager with an upbeat attitude toward others, Eddie has a unique ability to find the best in everyone. With a heart for people, Eddie uses his faith experiences as his guide to help others feel inspired and motivated.

Eddie is a native of Jacksonville, Florida, where he grew up in a single-family home with two other siblings. With a mother determined to see him make the best of his life, Eddie grew up with a foundation built on knowing and loving God, caring for others, gratitude, and discipline.

Eddie is a graduate of Florida State University, where, in 1994, he received a Bachelor of Science Degree in Accounting. With twenty-three years working in leadership roles in professional credit management and accounts receivables, Eddie spent twenty of those years with the same company, where he went from being a Credit Trainee to Regional Credit Manager.

After defining his purpose in 2017, it became clear that the assignment God had given him to share his faith testimony and God's blessings in his book, *Passing the Test of Faith*, needed to be completed.

Eddie is a strong believer that we are blessed in various ways so that we can be a blessing to others. He has served on the board of directors for the Pediatric Brain Tumor Foundation – Georgia Chapter and is actively involved in his church.

He resides in Alpharetta, GA, and is the father of four: Kendall, Kennedy, Christian, and Cameron. You can contact and learn more about Eddie by visiting his website at www.EddieLJohnson.com.

ACKNOWLEDGMENTS

With special thanks:

To Kennedy, Christian, and Cameron, you are indeed my faith reward, and I love you dearly. Regardless of what experiences you have in life, never stop trusting God. He loves you too much to turn his back on you.

To my mother, Beneva, for pouring your love into me and blessing me so richly with all the Godly wisdom shared throughout my life.

To my father, Eddie, Sr., for being there when I needed you most, for using your voice for God as an example for me to see a man who loves the Lord.

To my friend and pastor from a distance, Rev. Eddy J. Moise, Jr., for writing the foreword for this book and being an accountability partner for many years.

To Lisa Rahmings, Carlton Brannon, LaVetta Vann-Davis, Darlene Vann, and Vinnie Morris, for always being there in my most challenging times, believing in me, and not allowing me to forget why I needed to write this book.

To Renee and Dwayne Bradford, Sylvia Daniels, Rev. Ernest Glenn, and all my prayer warriors, for your continued prayers, love, friendship, and the feedback you provided for this book.

To my pastor, Rev. Dr. Michael T. McQueen, and the uplifting men in my life, for being examples of kingdom living, mentors, and positive men who do not mind sharing their love for God.

To Josie Selassie and James C. Hunter, your timing while working on this book could not have been any better. Thank you for your, caring hearts, advice and feedback.

To Donna Mosher, Cynthia Tucker, Kimberly Stephens, Syretta Ziegler, and Damon Peebles, for the dedicated time, service, and professional skills you provided me in completing this book.

To my publishing team at JETLAUNCH, Chris O'Byrne (President), Debbie O'Byrne, and Rae Kuddle (Design Experts), your support and feedback were excellent. Thank you for helping make this book a reality.

Thank you to all who have prayed or offered me an encouraging word over the years that I have been working on this book. You have all made a difference in my life.